THE STORY OF THE FOREST

A children's history of the Forest of Dean

New Venture Freemine

Andy Seed

Illustrated by Ursula Hurst

Acknowledgements

Many thanks to the people who have given their generous support to this project, in particular Cheryl Mayo, Geoff Davis of the Sungreen website, and David Harris for their considerable work in supplying photos.

Helen Chick, Forestry England

Rich Daniels, Hopewell Colliery

Jodie Hughes and Simon Lusted, Lydbrook Primary School

Averil Kear

Bernard Kear

Sue Middleton, Foresters' Forest

John Powell

Ian Standing

Chris Sullivan

Mary Sullivan, Chair, and Committee of the FoD Local History Society

Keith Walker

Jonathan Wright, Clearwell Caves

Nicola Wynn and the staff of Dean Heritage Centre

Forest of Dean Family History Trust

Robin Jackson and all at Worcestershire Archaeology, especially Steve Rigby for his reconstruction illustrations

Thanks also to everyone who contributed images (listed in credits on pages 58-59)

Text © Andy Seed 2021; illustrations © Ursula Hurst 2021

Editor: Simon Adams

Designer: Sarah Fountain, **fountaincreative.co.uk**

Published by the Forest of Dean Local History Society (**www.forestofdeanhistory.org.uk**) in association with Foresters' Forest, a National Lottery Heritage Funded Landscape Partnership Programme.

All rights reserved. No part of this book may be reproduced, stored in a retrieval system, or transmitted in any form or by any means, electronic, mechanical, photocopying, recording, or otherwise, without the prior written permission of the publisher.

Funded by

Contents

Introduction	4
Map of the Forest	6
A Forest timeline	8
Ancient times	22
A royal forest	24
Iron in the hills	26
Trees and timber	30
Coal	34
Living in the Forest	38
Transport and travel	42
Poverty	44
The Forest at war	46
Crime and punishment	48
Other industries	50
Entertainment and community events	51
Schools and education	52
HOOF	53
Tourism	54
Notable people	55
Places to visit	56
Forest dialect	57

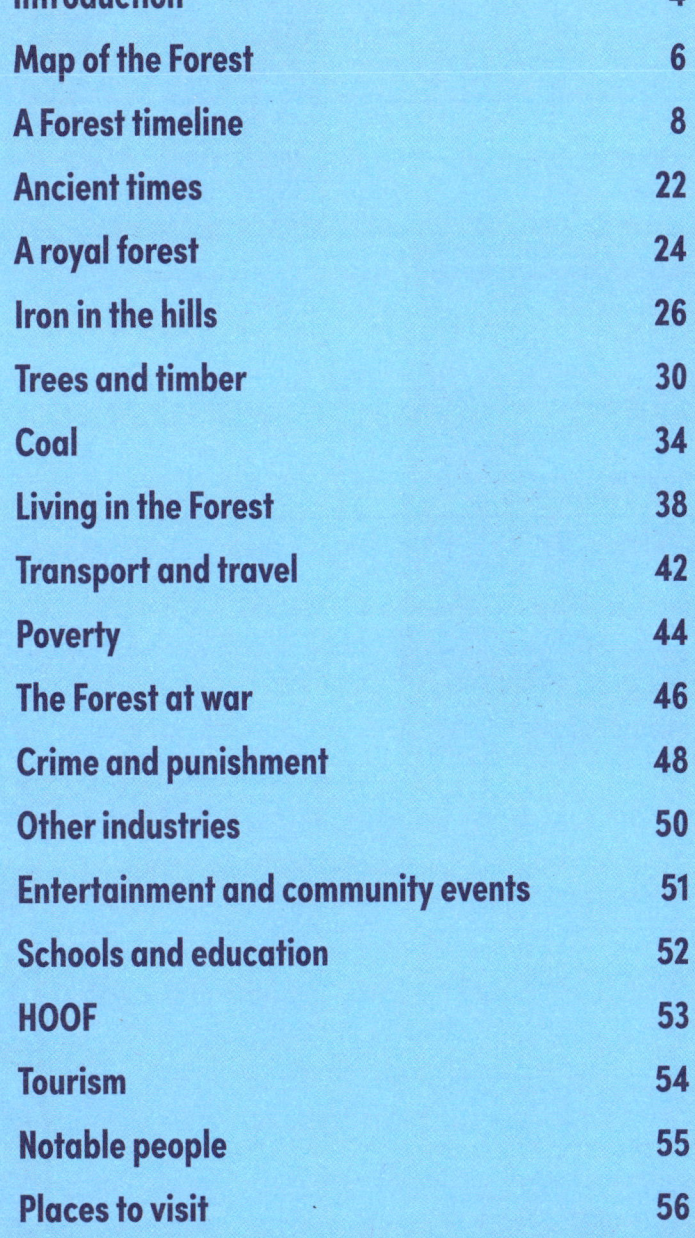

Introduction

The Forest of Dean is a place of secrets. Deep beneath the trees and red-rock valleys are hidden tunnels and ghostly passages. Among the beech-wooded hills you'll find mysterious towers, moss-covered ruins and buried rails. Everywhere there are ancient tracks, once trodden by strange Celtic tribes and Roman soldiers.

People came to the Forest for its riches: iron, coal and timber. Kings came to hunt its wild beasts. Following the warriors and hunters came poachers, miners, foresters, iron-makers, child labourers, and sheep badgers with their animals. Blazing furnaces made iron for wars, woodcutters felled the mighty oaks for great ships and tunnelling colliers went deep into the earth to bring up coal for the age of steam.

But none of this was easy. Battles were fought. There was danger, hunger, protest and riot. The woodland was stolen, smoking chimneys went up, and sprawling mines with great heaps of spoil choked the Forest's valleys. Those who worked down the dark pits built clusters of crude little cabins which later became stone villages clinging to the hillsides.

Now the big mines are no more. The Forest is quiet again. The glorious trees are back and among them, only the ghosts of the past remain.

4

Why care about history?

All that we are, all that we see around us, is built on the past. By discovering and uncovering what happened before our time, we learn more about ourselves as Foresters. We come to know our ancestors and find out what our great-great-grandparents went through, and their families before them.

They were once the guardians of the Dean. Now it is you.

This book will reveal some of the Forest's secrets, but my hope is that you will go on to discover many more – and have fun doing it!

Andy Seed June 2021

A Forest Timeline

9000–4000 BC
Stone Age

People: Hunter-gatherers
Animals: Large mammals included wolf, beaver, boar and deer

Ten thousand years ago, the Forest was thickly wooded. People hunted animals with spears and bows and arrows, using the skins to make simple clothes. They also gathered nuts and fruit, and fished the two rivers with nets and harpoons. Homes were simple, temporary stick huts. These shelters were made as groups moved around the Forest in search of food, which they cut up with flint tools, and cooked on open fires.

Things people didn't have
- ★ Metal
- ★ Cloth
- ★ Pottery
- ★ Crops
- ★ Farm animals
- ★ Permanent buildings
- ★ Villages

Imagine having to go out and find food every day. There were no shops in the Stone Age!

Evidence
Stone tools from this period have been dug up in the Forest.

A flint arrowhead found locally

9000–4000 BC Stone Age | 4000–2500 BC Late Stone Age | 2500–800 BC Bronze Age

2500–800 BC
Bronze Age

People: First settlers and farmers
Key discovery: People learned how to make bronze by mixing copper and tin found in rocks. This allowed them to make metal tools and weapons.

People cleared areas of the Forest and built small settlements of circular houses. They discovered how to grow crops, such as barley, and keep animals as livestock, and so became farmers. Fields were small and trees were cut down to make fences for sheep and cattle.

From around 1900 BC, the Beaker Folk came from Europe in boats and brought pottery. People became traders and lived in clans or families, ruled over by powerful chiefs. Weaving to make cloth was developed and craft workers created jewellery and bronze tools to trade.

Reproduction Bronze sword

Things people didn't have
- ★ Bricks
- ★ Cabbages
- ★ Rabbits
- ★ Domestic cats
- ★ Coins (until late Bronze Age)
- ★ Wheeled carts (until late Bronze Age)

How did people pay for things without money?

Evidence
Bronze tools have been discovered around the Forest. There are also standing stones and burial mounds which can still be seen.

The Staunton Longstone, near Coleford

8

around 600 BC
Iron Age

People: Tribes and settlers
Key discovery: People found iron in local rocks, which could be made into very strong tools, weapons and other useful objects (see pages 26-29).

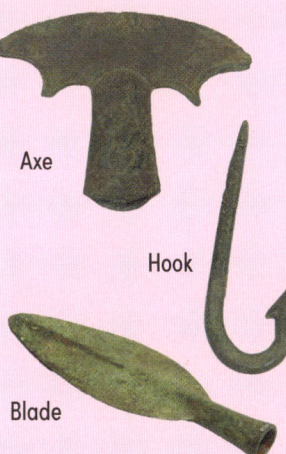
Axe
Hook
Blade

Settlers called Celts arrived from Europe and settled in and around the Forest. They were skilled metal workers with strong iron weapons. People lived in tribes and built large hill forts to protect themselves and to stop warriors from stealing cattle and food. There were forts or camps at Soudley, Symonds Yat and other places.

Farming methods improved and people kept geese, goats, pigs, sheep and cows. They made pottery using wheels, and used carts and chariots pulled by horses. Houses were round buildings with a single large room.

Things people didn't have
★ Towns
★ A system of money
★ Paved roads
★ Tiled roofs
★ Reading and writing
★ Calendars

Evidence
Hill forts and their earthworks can still be seen. Iron Age coins and pottery has been dug up around the Forest.

A gold stater coin found near Newent

600 BC Iron Age

What if another tribe stole your cattle? Would you go and fight to get them back (and risk death or becoming a slave), or would you take the hit?

Iron Age Hill Fort

9

75AD – 900s

75 AD The Romans

410 The Romans leave Britain

around 75 AD
The Romans

People: A mix of tribes (Ancient Britons) and soldiers (Romans)

Invasion! The Romans controlled a huge empire across Europe and North Africa. They invaded Britain in AD 43 with a strong army of trained soldiers.

Many of the British tribes, such as the Silures in this area, fought the invaders in fierce battles but the Roman armies were too strong and well armed.

They sent forces west into what is now the Forest, building roads and forts, and towns with strong stone and brick buildings.

The Romans made use of the Forest's rich reserves of iron ore and controlled the area from their base in the town of Glevum (Gloucester). As well as roads the Romans built villas, temples and marketplaces and introduced developments like baths, heating and sewage systems. They also used money in the form of coins and brought reading and writing. They stayed in the area for more than 300 years.

Things people didn't have
★ Clocks
★ Compasses
★ Banknotes
★ Gunpowder
★ Toilet paper
★ Windmills
★ Sugar

Remains of Roman buildings, for example this temple at Lydney Park, built in AD 370

What else do you think the Romans took from the Forest apart from iron?

Evidence
Roman objects found by archaeologists, for example, coins and a Roman dog sculpture found at Lydney

10

410
The Romans leave Britain

500 Angles and Saxons

Offa's Dyke had a ditch and a steep bank of earth

Powys — Wales
Mercia — England

790 Offa's Dyke

Offa was the Saxon king of Mercia, a kingdom in central England. Around 790 he built a long earthwork up to 8m high along the border between his land and the kingdom of Powys in Wales. This passed along the border of the Forest near the River Wye and can still be seen today.

around 500 Angles and Saxons

People: New settlers and raiders

People called Angles and Saxons began to arrive from northern Europe and settle in Britain. Some came to live in the Forest. They were farmers and skilled in woodwork. People lived in wooden houses made from the Forest's trees. They also mined for iron to make tools and weapons.

The Anglo-Saxons gradually mixed with other tribes and began to change the language spoken, bringing new words. At this time, children had to work and help with growing and preparing food, finding fuel and other jobs.

790 Offa's Dyke

900s A Royal Forest

Would you rather go to school each day or do work such as cleaning, fetching water, weaving, ploughing and weeding like Anglo-Saxon children had to do?

900s Royal hunting

Strong Saxon kings began to rule over large kingdoms until eventually they could be called Kings of England, such as Athelstan (king from 927–939). It is thought that some of the later kings hunted in the Forest of Dean for deer

Athelstan

Things people didn't have
★ Shops
★ Schools for everyone
★ Football
★ Castles
★ Cannons
★ Guns
★ Printing

Evidence

The remains of Offa's dyke

11

1066 - 1280

1066
The Normans

People: Mainly farmers

More invaders! In 1066 William the Conqueror sailed from France with a large Norman army and defeated the Saxon king Harold II at the Battle of Hastings. He became King William I of England and took over the whole country, including the Forest of Dean.

A royal forest
The Norman rulers saw the woods and open land of the Forest as valuable, so they established it as a royal forest owned by the king. The Normans spent Christmas at Gloucester and went hunting in the Forest. Special forest laws were put in place to protect the animals, trees and minerals, such as iron (see page 25).

1085 The Domesday Book

The Forest's deer and boar were an important source of meat for the royal table

1085
The Domesday Book

King William I ordered that a record should be made of all his land. Everything was written in the great Domesday Book, which lists villages around the Forest such as Mitcheldean and Ruardean. The Forest became known as the Forest of Dean (or Dene) around this time, although no one knows for certain where the name comes from.

Things people didn't have
★ Police
★ Theatres
★ Flushing toilets
★ Glass windows
★ Forks
★ Spectacles
★ Potatoes, rice and pasta

William I

1066 The Normans

St Briavels Castle as it might have looked in the Middle Ages

Evidence
★ Remains of castles built by the Normans, such as St Briavels
★ Written documents, such as the Domesday Book

The Forest was valuable because of its deer and boar, but why else do you think it was very important to the king?

12

around 1200
Late Middle Ages

People: Villagers, miners and farmers

A hard life: At this time people were often known by the jobs they did, for example John the miller or Thomas the fisher. Most people were poor farmworkers called peasants. Their life was hard and they had to work for a master.

The Forest's large deposits of iron were very important at this time. The king not only earned income from rents paid for mines on royal land, but rulers like Henry II fought many wars and so needed iron for weapons and armour.

Knight in armour

1217
Charter of the Forest

Laws were put in place to protect the deer. People were not allowed to hunt, use dogs or fell trees on royal land. Despite this, poaching was still common and the Forest's wild boar had gone by 1300.

1253
Freeminers

In this year, 20 iron miners from the Forest helped King Henry III fight in France. They were used as expert engineers, able to tunnel under walls and castle defences. Later, Forest miners helped other kings in the same way. As a result, miners born in the Forest could claim special rights as Freeminers. For example, they were allowed to take wood from the forest for their mine workings (see page 26).

Henry III

The Miners' Brass can be seen in Newland church.

1275
New villages

No one was allowed to live in the Forest, apart from officials who guarded it, but villages began to grow up around the edges of the woodland, such as Coleford.

1280
The last wolves

It is thought that the last wolf in the Forest was killed around this time, after King Edward I ordered the destruction of all wolves in his kingdom.

13

1348 - 1600

1600 Blast Furnaces

The Black Death caused boils and swellings on the body

1348
The Black Death

A terrible outbreak of plague killed over a quarter of all people in England. It is not known how badly the Forest was affected but many hundreds of people must have died.

Things people didn't have
- Bedrooms
- Bathrooms
- Telescopes
- Accurate maps
- Newspapers
- Oranges
- Coffee

Evidence
- Remains of mine workings from the time.
- Written documents such as the Charter of the Forest.
- Objects and buildings

A medieval axe head from the Forest

A Medieval village

1348 The Black Death

What would be the worst thing about being a peasant in these medieval times?

1485
The Tudors

People: More people of the Forest were involved in mining.

Henry VIII

Elizabeth I

Walter Raleigh

Meat for the monarchs: The Tudor kings and queens less often used forests for hunting, but Dean was still important for supplying the court with venison (deer meat).

1500s
Oaks for ships

King Henry VIII began building wooden ships for an English navy at this time. Then, during the reign of Queen Elizabeth I, sailors such as Francis Drake and Walter Raleigh started to bring back gold and treasure from long voyages to America, where they raided Spanish ships and settlements. The Forest became important for supplying oak timbers for ship building.

Drake's Golden Hinde

1600
Blast furnaces

The number of iron mines in the Forest grew as it became England's main source of iron. An improvement in technology came around the year 1600, when blast furnaces were introduced at places with streams, such as Soudley (see page 28).

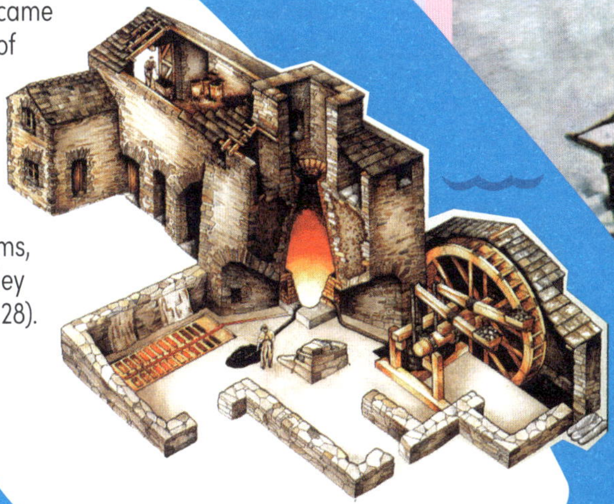

Early blast furnace

Things people didn't have
★ Factories
★ Steam engines
★ Cookers
★ Fridges
★ Pianos
★ Tomatoes
★ Chocolate bars

Evidence
★ Written documents, for example orders for ship's timbers
★ Paintings and drawings of Tudor ships
★ Objects from the period such as weapons, tools and furniture

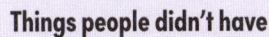
Tudor written document

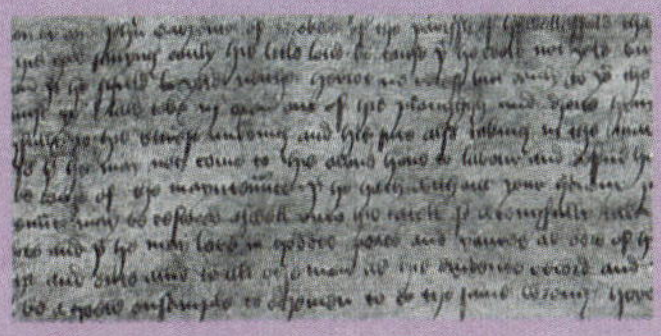

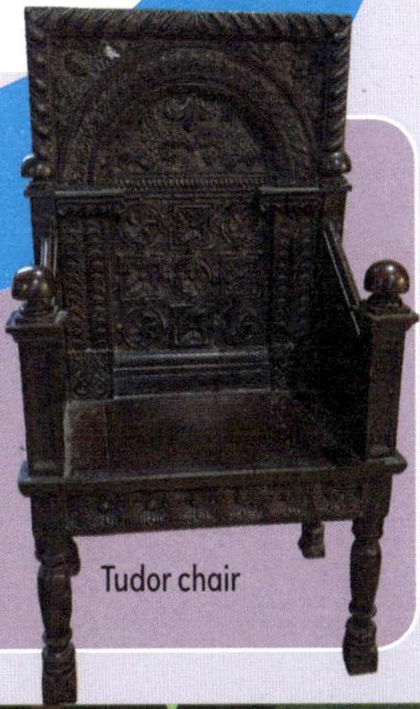

Tudor chair

Why do you think that some visitors at this time described the people of the Forest as "wild and brutal"?

15

1603 – 1837

1603
The Stuarts and Georgians

People: Many were involved in mining and iron-making. There was a great difference between the lives of rich and poor, with poorer people often suffering from starvation.

A time of change: Much of the ancient woodland was cut down in this period to make fuel for the growing iron industry in the Forest. The population grew as jobs increased, and miners along with quarrymen began to build small cabins on the edge of the Forest and pasture their sheep, pigs and cows on royal land (sometimes called Crown land).

It was also a time of war, riots and conflict. When the rulers started to inclose (build walls around or fence off) large parts of the Forest, Freeminers and other local people became angry that they couldn't collect wood and let their animals roam.

Things people didn't have
★ Cars
★ Electricity in homes
★ Telephones
★ Baked beans
★ Films
★ Typewriters
★ Bikes

Was it best that trees were protected for making ships or that local miners could use them to shore up their mines to stop the tunnels collapsing?

1612
The King's Ironworks

King James I allows a 'King's Ironworks' to be set up by wealthy men to control the production of iron and to make money. The Freeminers object strongly to this. There are also riots in 1631 after parts of the Forest are granted to government officials and rich landowners for their estates.

1638
Sir John Winter

King Charles I sells nearly all of the Forest's woodland to a rich ironmaker called Sir John Winter (or Wintour) of Lydney. Winter cuts down most of the trees and builds fences which the Foresters tear down.

Charles I

1642–51
English Civil War

The war across England between parliament and the king comes to the Forest. There is a small battle in Coleford in 1643. The war saves the Forest from being destroyed by Sir John Winter, who flees when the king's armies are defeated.

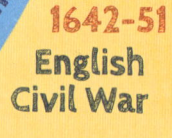

Civil War soldier

1660
The Dean Forest Act

The English navy demands that the Forest should supply more timber to build ships. A law is passed and in 1668, 4,452 hectares (11,000 acres) of woodland are inclosed for planting new oaks. Many ironworks are removed along with hundreds of illegal squatters now living on land belonging to the Crown.

Timeline: 1603 The Stuarts and Georgians · 1612 The King's Ironworks · 1638 Sir John Winter · 1642-51 English Civil War · 1660 The Dean Forest Act · 1676 Speech House

16

1676
Speech House is built as one of six lodges to house wardens protecting the Forest. It also included a courtroom.

Early image of Speech House

1700s
Encroachment

People once again begin to build cabins and small cottages on the edge of the Forest as laws are not strictly enforced.

Coal mining increases in the Forest as new pits are opened.

1795
Bread riots

There is a shortage of bread as the government buys up grain for the army, which is fighting the French military leader Napoleon in Europe. Many miners' families begin to starve, and two men are hanged for stealing flour.

1700s Encroachment — 1795 The Industrial Revolution arrives — 1795 Bread riots — 1802 Nelson and the Forest — 1816 The first church — 1831 The Dean Forest Riots

1795
The Industrial revolution arrives

The first steam engine in the Forest is used to make iron at a blast furnace in Cinderford. Horse-drawn railways called tramroads are also built at this time to transport coal to the River Wye.

Plaque in the centre of the Forest

1802
Nelson and the Forest

Admiral Lord Nelson visits the area and writes a report, asking why Forest timber supplies to build ships for the navy are so low. It results in inclosures (fenced off areas) and the planting of millions of acorns. The trees were never used because iron warships took over. (see page 31)

1816
New churches

Christ Church at Berry Hill is the first church built in the Forest for centuries. Many others follow in the 1800s.

1831
The Dean Forest Riots

Miner Warren James is sentenced to death for leading a mob which tore down the fences of the inclosures. (see page 49)

Plaque at the Angel Hotel in Coleford

THROUGH THIS ARCHWAY WARREN JAMES THE LEADER OF THE FORESTERS IN THE DEAN RIOTS WAS BROUGHT ON 15 JUNE 1831 AFTER HIS CAPTURE — ERECTED BY THE FOREST OF DEAN LOCAL HISTORY SOCIETY

Evidence
Remains of things built at the time.

Written documents: records of laws and crimes, for example:

17

1837 – 1900

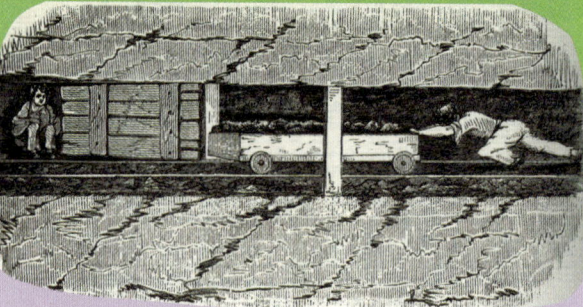

1837
Victorian times

People: Mining for coal and iron dominated the Forest at this time and thousands of people depended on the mines for a living. It was an age of smoke, steam and dirt.

1838
Mining expands rapidly

Children in a mine

A new law reduces the rights of Freeminers and allows outsiders to buy and control mines. Larger deep-coal mines are created, and houses are built for new workers as the industry grows. In 1842 another law stops children under 10 being employed underground.

The growth of towns and villages: The Forest's communities grew very quickly at this time as people came to live in the area to work in the mines, as well as in factories, shops and other businesses.

An early terrace in Cinderford

Fallow deer

Imagine working deep underground in a mine every day as a child, pulling heavy coal trucks in cramped, dark tunnels.

Timeline:
- 1837 Victorian times
- 1838 Mining expands rapidly
- 1844 Homes made legal
- 1850 Deer are killed
- 1854 The first railway
- 1870s New schools

1844
Homes made legal
Houses built on Forest land are no longer unlawful.

1850
Deer are killed
All fallow deer in the Forest are destroyed to put an end to poaching.

1854
The first railway
The Forest's first steam railway is a goods line, opened to take coal, iron, stone and timber to the docks at Bullo Pill on the River Severn.

1871
The first local newspaper
The *Dean Forest Guardian* is launched. This eventually becomes today's *The Forester*.

1870s
New schools
Most of the Forest's schools were built in this period, and many children received an education for the first time.

The Severn Railway Bridge

Evidence
★ Buildings.
★ Written documents such as newspapers, letters and police reports.

1879
A bridge across the Severn
New rail lines are added across the Forest and an iron railway bridge is built from Purton to Sharpness, 1,269m in length.

1885
The first street lights
Gas lamps are first used to light some of Cinderford's streets.

1871
The first local newspaper

Things people didn't have
★ Radios
★ Vacuum cleaners
★ Chainsaws
★ Aeroplanes
★ Teddy bears
★ Coca Cola
★ Ice cream sellers

1889
Who killed the bears?
A group of travelling Frenchmen with two performing bears are attacked by a mob near Ruardean. The bears were killed after a false rumour had started that they had mauled local women and children.

1898
Coal is king
The Forest's collieries produce one million tonnes of coal. Iron mining is in steep decline, with Cinderford's ironworks closing in 1894.

1898
Sheep everywhere
Many miners followed the custom of commoning (keeping) animals in the Forest, with the total number of sheep over 10,000.

Foxes Bridge Colliery near Cinderford

19

1901 – The 21st Century

1901
The 20th Century and beyond

People: Mining declines as coal becomes too expensive to extract. Collieries close and other traditional industries with them, meaning that many Foresters have to leave the Dean to find work.

War and more: The 1900s will always be remembered as the century of two world wars but also a time when people's standard of living improved and ordinary families could own a car and start to travel more.

The Downham family of Bream in 1939

1914-18
World War I

Many Forest men joined the armed forces and lost their lives in the war, including miners who helped to dig tunnels under enemy positions.

The war memorial at Drybrook Memorial Hall.

Timeline:
- 1901 The 20th Century
- 1914-18 World War I
- 1924 The Forestry Commission
- 1926 The National Strike
- 1929 Tolkien visits the Forest
- 1935 Birth of Dennis Potter
- 1939-45 World War II
- 1947 Coal mines nationalised

1924
The Forestry Commission

The newly created Forestry Commission takes over the running of the Forest of Dean.

1926
The National Strike

Coal miners faced longer hours and cuts in wages, set by the mine owners. The miners went on strike for seven months, suffering terrible poverty and starvation. A hunger march was organised to the workhouse in Westbury to try and obtain help and relief.

1929
JRR Tolkien visits the Forest

The writer JRR Tolkien helped archaeologists to excavate the Roman Temple at Lydney Park. Some say that this experience may have inspired him when writing *The Hobbit* and *The Lord of the Rings*.

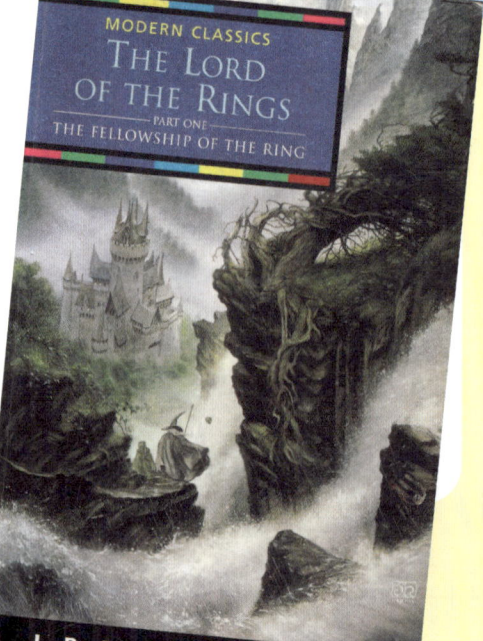

1935
Dennis Potter born near Berry Hill

Dennis Potter went on to write some of the most famous dramas shown on television.

1938
National Forest Park
The Forest of Dean becomes a National Forest Park for people to visit.

1947
Coal mines nationalised
There are only six deep mines left in the Forest and all are taken over by the government.

1948
The NHS
The National Health Service begins. For the first time ever, Forest families do not have to worry about paying to see a doctor.

1965
The end of the Forest coal industry
Northern United, the last deep coal mine in the Forest, is closed with the loss of jobs. A small number of Freeminers continue to work in their own pits across the Forest.

The hooter which signalled the shifts at Northern United Colliery.

1939-45
World War II
Factories in the Forest help the war effort, and the woodlands are used to hide ammunition. Prisoner-of-war camps are built. Once more many Foresters die fighting for their country. (see page 47)

This factory at Lydbrook made cables used in World War I and fuel pipelines used in World War II. Iron mining in the Forest also stopped in 1945.

1960
The Severn Railway Bridge disaster
Two large oil tankers collide with the bridge's support piers in thick fog on the River Severn (see page 42).

1974
A Child in the Forest
Winifred Foley's memories of growing up in the Forest in Brierley are broadcast on BBC Radio and her popular book *A Child in the Forest* follows (see page 55).

1948 The NHS — **1960** The Severn Railway Bridge disaster — **1965** The end of the Forest coal industry — **1974** A Child in the Forest — **1974** A young JK Rowling — **1983** The Dean Heritage Centre — **1986** Sculpture Trail — **2011** HOOF

1974
A young JK Rowling
The author of the hugely popular Harry Potter books moves to Tutshill, just outside the Forest, aged nine. She goes on to attend Wyedean School in Sedbury.

1983
The Dean Heritage Centre
The Dean Heritage Centre opens in Soudley, telling the remarkable story of the Forest's history.

1986
Sculpture Trail
The Forest of Dean Sculpture Trail is created, bringing thousands of visitors to the area.

2011
HOOF
1,000 people gather at Speech House to protest at government plans to sell the UK's forests, under the banner of **Hands Off Our Forest** (HOOF). The campaign is successful and later **Foresters' Forest** is begun, helping people to cherish all that the Forest has to offer (see page 53).

JK Rowling

Ancient Times

It is not known how long there has been a forest in this area but we do know that the woodlands date back thousands of years. We also know that early settlers came here in the Stone Age, because flint tools have been found dating back to Neolithic times (around 10,000 years ago).

These first settlers were hunter-gatherers. They lived around the edges of the forest and began to form clearings as they cut down trees to make wooden tools or shelters, or use for fuel.

Why did these early people live around woodlands?

Before the age of shops and houses with central heating, people's lives were taken up with finding three things:

1. Food
2. Shelter
3. Warmth

The Forest could supply these:

Food: Deer and boar to hunt, fish from the two rivers, plus acorns and beech nuts to feed the settlers' animals.

Shelter: Caves in the hills, and also a supply of branches and sticks to build simple homes and fences.

Warmth: Wood to burn and to make fires to cook on.

What's in the cave?

King Arthur's Cave near Symond's Yat has been used for thousands of years and not just by people. Archaeologists have dug into the floor of the cave and discovered the remains of these animals:

★ Bear
★ Hyena
★ Woolly Mammoth
★ Lion
★ Woolly rhinoceros

A cave hyena

King Arthur's Cave

The iron age fort at Symond's Yat had a strong defensive position high above the River Wye

The age of tribes

The settlers of the Forest became farmers. They made bigger clearings in the trees over time and began to plant crops to eat and to keep more animals, including cattle. They built larger houses and discovered how to make metal to create tools and weapons. The Forest supplied both ore (rocks full of iron) and the charcoal needed to heat it to extract the metal.

As time went on people lived in tribes or clans, ruled over by strong chieftains. Settlers arrived from other lands and mixed with the Ancient Britons. Many tribes built hill forts to protect themselves and their animals from attack by others. The remains of these forts can be seen in the Forest today.

Watch out, it's the Romans!

The strongest and best-organised settlers in ancient times were the Romans. They were very good at all kinds of things, including:

★ Fighting
★ Building
★ Making roads
★ Bringing new ideas
★ Introducing new foods
★ Creating towns such as Glevum (Gloucester)

Roman activity in the Forest of Dean

The Romans used the rivers to transport people and goods and they used timber from the woods for building. They also mined local iron ore for making iron for weapons, tools, nails and more.

Detector discovery

In 2012 Gavin Warren was walking through a field in Yorkley when his metal detector made a sound. Digging down he found a scattered hoard of 499 Roman coins dating from the years AD 295–340. The coins are now on display at Dean Heritage Centre in Soudley. No one knows why they were buried but here are three possibilities:

★ They were a person's savings, kept in a safe place
★ They were left as an offering to a god
★ They were hidden during dangerous times

Some other Roman hoards found in the Forest of Dean

★ 3,000 coins found at Perry Grove in 1848
★ Over 1,000 coins found near Coleford in 1852
★ 155 silver coins found near Bream in 1854
★ 250 coins found at Woolaston in 1887
★ Over 18,000 coins found near Lydbrook in 1895
★ 500 coins found at Oldcroft in 1991

Some of the Roman coins found at Yorkley [please note that metal detecting in the Forest is now against the law]

23

A Royal Forest

Six hundred years after the Romans departed, the Forest was mostly a thickly wooded area with people working in it mining, iron-making, cutting timber for charcoal and collecting bark.

It is not known when exactly the Forest of Dean became a royal hunting ground, but it was probably at the time of the later Anglo-Saxon kings such as Edward the Confessor, who ruled England from 1042–1066. The Norman kings who followed enjoyed meat from the Forest and they also enjoyed the money the land brought them, from activities like mining and iron-making.

A medieval deer hunt

100 boar were ordered for a Christmas feast in 1254!

The Conqueror's Forest

After winning the Battle of Hastings, the Norman King William I controlled all of the Royal Forests of England. His rule changed the Forest of Dean in a number of ways:

★ It was made larger
★ Laws were put in place to protect the deer and boar, with harsh punishments for poaching
★ The Forest became a kind of royal nature reserve so meat could be supplied to the court and hunting could be enjoyed by the King and his nobles

What is a Forest?

Today we think of a forest as woodland, but the word originally meant an area of land governed by special forest laws where only the king was allowed to hunt. A forest could include land without trees such as fields, pasture and waste ground.

Bigger and Smaller

The boundaries of the Forest have changed a lot through history. In Norman times, it was much larger than it is now.

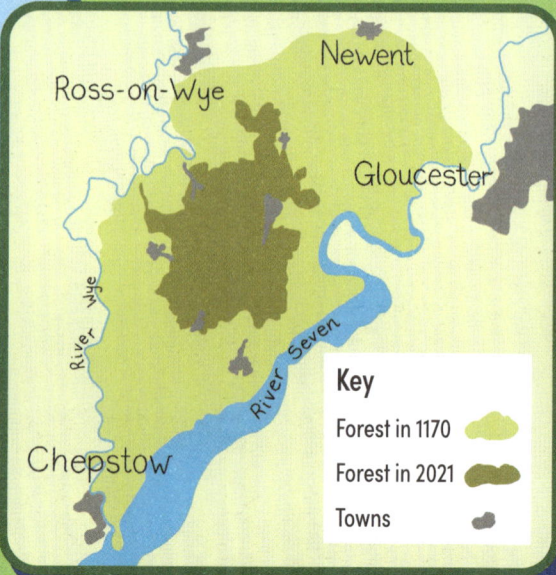

Key
Forest in 1170
Forest in 2021
Towns

24

St Briavels Castle is now a youth hostel

The beasts of the hunt

Deer provided venison (meat) for the royal table and were carefully protected. Fallow deer are the main species seen in the Forest today, but in the Middle Ages red deer and roe deer were also plentiful. The king and his nobles would hunt them with horses and dogs, using a bow and arrow for the kill.

Female roe deer

Wild boar were large, fierce animals, dangerous to hunt because they would sometimes fight back and could kill a dog with their powerful bite. For this reason, it is thought they would be killed with spears. The boar found in the Forest today are the result of farm animals escaping or being released into the woods, as the true wild boar had all gone by the year 1300.

Medieval wild boar

Boar found in the forest today

Forest Law

In the 1100s a King's Warden was appointed, based at St Briavels Castle, which became the centre for the management of the Forest. The Warden had a number of officers to help enforce forest law. These laws made sure that the crown (the rulers) benefitted fully from the Forest's resources of land, wood, animals, and minerals such as iron.

The officers included:

Verderers
Verderers were in charge of protecting the vert (woodlands) and venison (deer) of the Forest. There are still four Verderers today who meet four times a year at Speech House – the role has been going for over 800 years!

Gaveller
The Gaveller was the officer in charge of the Forest's mines, responsible for collecting payments from miners. There is still a Deputy Gaveller who oversees freemining in the Forest today and keeps official documents. The current Deputy Gaveller is Dan Howell.

Regarders
These part-time officials walked the Forest's boundaries to check for cases of law-breaking, such as building on royal land.

Foresters-in-fee
Almost like Forest police, these men patrolled the woods and arrested offenders for crimes such as stealing the king's animals or taking wood without permission (see Crime and punishment, see page 48).

Later, in the 1600s, the Warden was replaced by a Deputy Surveyor, who manages the Forest for the crown. The current Deputy Surveyor is Kevin Stannard.

The current Verderers

A unique Forest
Nowhere else will you find Verderers, a Deputy Surveyor and Deputy Gaveller still working today. This is one of the things that makes the Forest of Dean special.

Iron in the hills

Beneath the Forest are many different types of rock, including the pink-coloured Old Red Sandstone which gives much local soil its colour. There is also a ring of grey limestone which comes to the surface in small cliffs, especially on the western side of the Forest. This rock contains iron in places and has been mined since before Roman times when Iron Age people discovered that the metal could be made into excellent tools and weapons.

Iron and Coal Measures

Key
Coal reserves
Main iron ore reserves

The mysterious scowles

At certain places around the Forest you will see strange, deep holes in the ground, many joined to form steep, dry gulleys separated by towers of rock. The two best known examples are Puzzlewood and the Devil's Chapel near Bream. These are 'scowles', once natural gaps in the local limestone that have been enlarged by people digging for iron ore since ancient times. They are now overgrown with trees, moss and ivy.

Freeminers

In medieval times, when wars were common, the kings of England were aware that the Forest's iron miners had three very valuable skills:

1. They were experts at digging defences before battles
2. They knew how to make enemy walls and buildings collapse by undermining them
3. Many were also skilled archers

As a result, many miners were taken along with the king's soldiers during wars against the French and the Scots. Their successes brought rewards, and the Forest miners became known as 'free miners' (written today as Freeminers). They were given special rights to take iron, stone, coal and other minerals from the Forest, along with wood. There are still a few Freeminers working in the Forest today – see page 37.

A nice little earner

When the area became a royal forest in the Middle Ages, kings made money from iron mines by charging rents to the miners who operated them. This continued for many centuries and by the 1600s the Forest was the most important iron-producing area in England.

How do you become a Freeminer?

Over time, rules were put in place to decide who could become a Freeminer, and these still mostly apply today. You had to:

★ Be born in the hundred of St Briavels (the old district where the Forest is located)
★ Be male
★ Be over 21
★ Have worked in a Forest mine for at least a year and a day

A BIG order

One of the most-deadly weapons used by medieval armies was the crossbow. This fired bolts called quarrels, which had a sharp iron point. A huge number of these were made at a special armoury at St Briavels Castle in the 1200s using iron mined in the Forest. In 1277 King Edward I ordered a staggering 200,000 quarrels for his battles against the Welsh rulers.

Girls can be miners too!

In 2009 a local woman called Elaine Morman, who mined at Clearwell, applied to register as a Freeminer. She was turned down because she was not male, but appealed against the decision and the matter was even talked over in parliament. Elaine was told the law could not be changed. However, Elaine was accepted as a Forest of Dean miner, showing that females can be miners too.

Elaine Morman

Iron ore

Slag

How iron is made

The rocks containing iron, called iron ore, were mined in the Forest for centuries and iron was also made locally. As time went on, the technology improved and different methods were used. All of these had a large effect on the landscape of the area.

Smelting

Smelting is the way that iron is released from the rocks it is found in. It is a chemical process that needs a lot of heat. The iron ore must be heated with carbon to at least 1,150°C. At that temperature the rocks melt and separate from the iron. The iron itself melts at 1,540°C and flows to collect under the rocky waste.

Fuel

The traditional fuel burnt to provide the heat was charcoal (see page 30 for how this was made). This also provides the carbon in the iron. Huge numbers of trees in the Forest were grown and cut down to make charcoal. In the 1800s and later, smelting was done using coke as a fuel. Coke was made from coal, also mined locally.

Slag

The waste material left over from smelting is called slag or cinders, and there are deposits of it all over the Forest. Because it has been melted in fire, it sometimes has a glassy, smooth look. Much of it contains traces of rust-coloured iron.

Furnaces, forges and foundries

Iron smelting in the Forest was done in furnaces where the ore could be heated to melting temperature. As time went on the technology improved resulting in more and better quality iron.

Bloomery

These small, simple furnaces were used for about 2,000 years, from Iron Age times. They look like a small chimney made from clay or stones, and each one produced a lump of iron called a bloom.

Charcoal blast furnace

By the year 1600, iron makers in the Forest were able to melt the metal so that it could be poured into a mould of any shape. This is called casting. The blast furnace achieved a higher temperature by blasting air into the burning charcoal using bellows powered by a water mill.

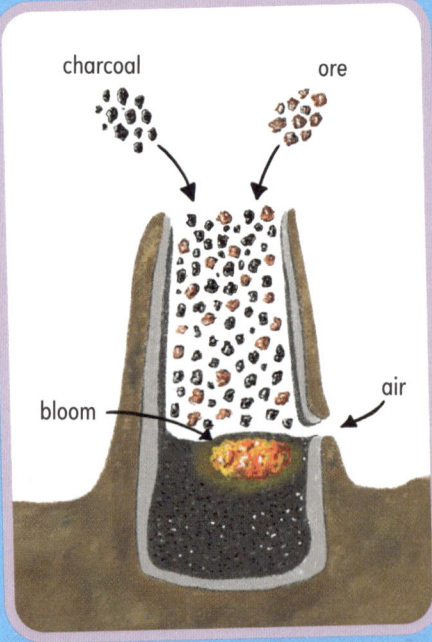

A bloomery furnace

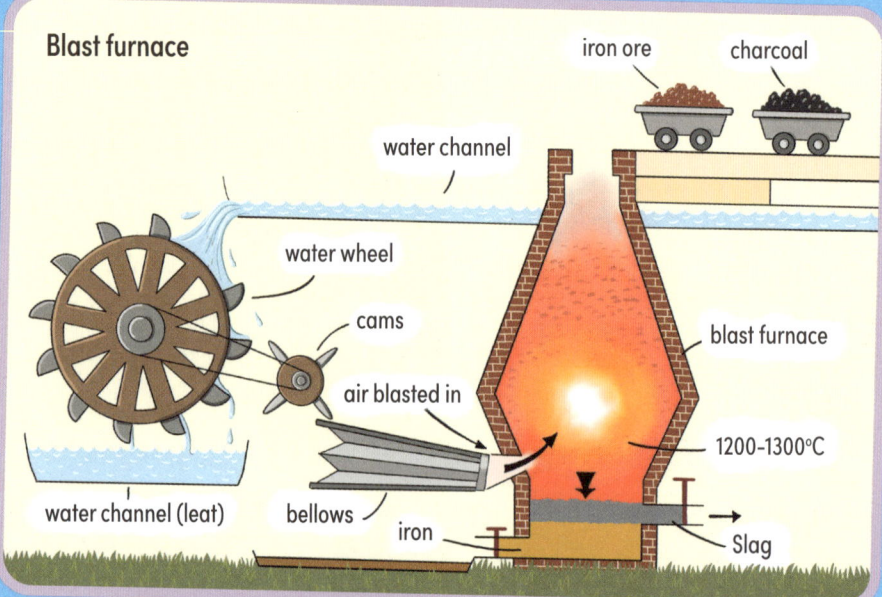

By the 1820s parts of the Forest such as Cinderford were full of heat, noise and smoke. Steam engines now powered the furnaces and allowed them to make 30 tons of iron a week.

Forest streams like Soudley Brook provided the energy to work these furnaces

Forges

The cast iron that was made in blast furnaces was often heated and hammered by smiths to make it into tougher wrought iron. This was done in noisy forges.

Foundries

Foundries are factories that make products from iron and steel. There were foundries around the Forest in the 1800s making things such as rails and wheels for trains.

The remains of Whitecliff Ironworks near Coleford can still be seen today

Working in an iron mine

At Clearwell Caves you can visit old iron mines and see the tunnels and huge underground hollows that the miners dug out by hand using pick axes. Have a look at these facts about iron mines and decide if you would be able to do the job:

Forest iron miners Mr Holder and his son in the 1850s, with nellies in their mouths

★ The working day was 10 hours with a 30–45-minute break for lunch (usually bread and cheese with cold tea to drink)
★ It was very dark: the only light came from candles held in the mouth using a 'nelly'
★ Children were given the job of carrying out the heavy rocks on their backs in baskets called billies (see page 36 for more about children working)

Some lost Forest iron mines

Several small iron mines were run by families who often gave them quirky names:

★ Crow's Nest
★ China Engine
★ Old Ham Pit
★ Speedwell New Bridge
★ Tingles Level
★ Old Sling Pot
★ Forget-me-not

★ There was a lot of crouching and crawling: the mines at Clearwell cover over 81 hectares (200 acres) and go 180m deep
★ There were no toilets but plenty of rats

The King's Ironworks

Trouble flared up in 1612 when King James I approved the setting up of the 'King's Ironworks' with four large furnaces, including one at Parkend. The plan was that all ore mined in the Forest should go to these works and that a section of the woodlands should be enclosed (fenced off) to provide charcoal for fuel. The freeminers were angry that this interfered with their long-held rights. This led to riots and the destruction of the fences.

Robert Mushet

A clever and important expert in metals called Robert Forester Mushet carried out experiments to make better steel in the 1800s at Darkhill Ironworks near Milkwall. In 1868 he discovered how to make a very hard steel that could be used for high quality cutting tools.

Robert Mushet

The decline of iron

In the 1800s, coal mining became more profitable than iron mining in the Forest and so many mines closed, especially when ore could be bought more cheaply from places such as Spain. Today the only mining carried out at Clearwell Caves is for a small amount of ochre: red and yellow powders that are used to colour paints among other uses.

Iron ore mined in the Forest of Dean	
Year	Tonnes
1860	192,074
1871	170,611
1877	79,646
1885	35,249
1901	9,769
1921	1,727

Ochre

Trees and timber

Nobody knows how many trees there are in the Forest today, but one estimate is around 20 million. In the past, trees were even more valuable than they are now. Before steel and concrete became available, wood was the essential material for building, transport, furniture, fuel for cooking and heating, and for industries such as charcoal making and ship building. While trees were being cut down to supply these needs, kings also wanted to maintain woodlands to protect the animals they hunted. No wonder the Forest of Dean was so important!

The Charter of the Forest

In 1217 King Henry III of England was only 10 years old! Some of his advisers thought it would be a good idea for the king to spell out what was allowed and not allowed in royal forests, including Dean. As a result, he signed a charter setting out different people's rights to use the forests to collect wood, graze their animals and more. It also put an end to the death penalty for poaching.

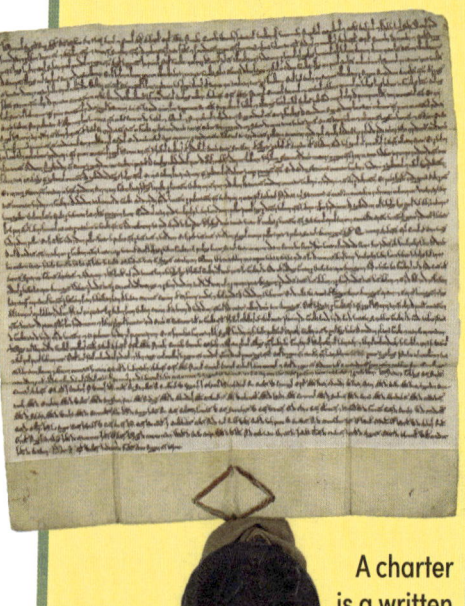

A charter is a written document

Charcoal: Fuel from the Forest

To make iron you need a lot of heat, and for centuries the fuel burnt to supply this was charcoal, made from wood. It was the only way to achieve the high temperatures needed to smelt ore and so it was in big demand, especially in the 1300s when the large number of wars meant that lots of iron was needed for weapons and armour.

How to make charcoal In medieval times large numbers of charcoal burners worked in the Forest carrying out the skilled job of 'cooking' wood so that it doesn't burn fully and turn to ash. They lived in small shelters next to their charcoal heaps. Here is how they worked:

1. Cut branches into pieces and leave to dry
2. Make a flue (a kind of chimney) using a tower of logs
3. Stack the pieces of wood carefully around the flue in a dome shape
4. Cover with turf and soil to keep the air out

5. Light the stack by dropping burning embers into the flue
6. Watch the stack for 3-5 days, checking the colour of the smoke
7. When the smoke turns blue, sprinkle the stack with water to put out the fire
8. Wait 24 hours then uncover the heap to collect the charcoal.

Coppicing

Charcoal-making uses a huge amount of wood (six tonnes makes one tonne of charcoal). This is one of the reasons that Forest trees were often coppiced, so that they kept producing new growth. Coppicing means cutting back a tree to near ground level so that it puts out lots of new stems.

A coppiced tree

Where are all the trees?

In the 1600s Sir John Winter paid the king an enormous pile of money for the right to control the Forest and operate ironworks. His men cut down most of the trees, which angered the Freeminers and other local people. Legend says that Winter was chased by soldiers during the Civil War and, on horseback, leapt off a high cliff above the River Wye to escape. This may not be true!

Why did people strip bark off trees?

Tree bark was another valuable product of the Forest in the past. Much of it was used by people called tanners to make leather. Bark contains chemicals which stop leather from rotting. Tanning was one of the stinkiest jobs in history, as leather was soaked in poo and urine to prepare it!

A medieval tanner

Ships vs Iron

England (and later Britain) developed a powerful navy during the 1500s, 1600s and 1700s, using wooden ships armed with heavy cannons to fight battles at sea. It took at least 2,000 oak trees to build a large warship and the Forest of Dean provided much of this timber. This led to lots of disputes with ironmakers in the Forest who needed wood to fire their furnaces:

HMS *Victory*

HMS *Victory* was the Royal Navy's finest warship of the late 1700s. It was a wooden sailing ship, built using oak, mainly from the Forest of Dean. *Victory* was Lord Nelson's flagship in the Battle of Trafalgar in 1805 against France and Spain. In 2004 two oak trees from the Forest were used to repair this famous ship at Portsmouth.

HMS *Victory*

Nelson lost an arm and an eye in sea battles, and was later shot on board HMS *Victory*

Nelson and the Forest

Admiral Lord Nelson was the legendary commander of the Royal Navy during Britain's wars with Napoleon, the French general. In 1802 Nelson passed through the Wye Valley and saw for himself how much Forest oak was available for building new warships. He was not happy and reported back that young trees were being destroyed by deer and sheep, and acorns gobbled by pigs. He demanded that oaks needed to be grown and protected for the future.

Inclosures again

Following Nelson's report in the early 1800s, once more a large part of the Forest was fenced off. An Act of Parliament was passed to protect trees for the navy and 4,452 hectares (11,000 acres) of the Forest were inclosed so that acorns could be planted and the young trees protected from grazing animals.

A woodcut of Warren James by Clifford Harper

What were inclosures?

An inclosure is an area of land fenced to keep animals and people off it. As well as fences, inclosures were sometimes made using stone walls or earth banks.

Inclosures = trouble

The inclosures caused a lot of anger in the Forest, as they had done in the past, and this led to serious riots, with fences being torn down and the rebels' leader Warren James being sentenced to death (see page 49). Why did the people of the Forest hate the inclosures? There are several reasons:

★ Many families were very poor and relied on being able to collect firewood and graze their animals in the Forest
★ Freeminers found it hard to make a living due to rich owners gaining control of mining in the Forest, helped by new inventions such as steam engines: the inclosures restricted the ancient rights of the Freeminers even more
★ Foresters felt that outsiders were taking away their special customs and freedoms
★ They felt that the fences were left up for too long

Freeminers used a lot of timber to shore up their mines, to stop tunnels collapsing

The changing face of forestry

Trees have been planted and cut down in the Forest for centuries, but the way these things have been done has changed enormously. Here is the story of tree felling in the Dean:

The 5,000-year-old Langdale axe head was found at Viney Hill

1. **Axe no questions**
   Chopping down a tree by hand is hard work! Prehistoric stone axes came first, followed by much better iron ones.

2. **They saw a faster way**
   When strong steel was developed in the 1800s, foresters used a two-man crosscut saw to fell trees. These were used in the Forest until the 1950s.

Horse power

Before the age of machines, felled logs were moved by horses. Animals have less impact on the environment than heavy vehicles, so are still used in some protected areas of woodland. They can also reach places that vehicles can't.

3. **The chain takes the strain**
   Felling became much quicker in the late 20th century, when chainsaws using petrol engines allowed one person to cut down a tree in less than a minute.

4. **Heavy-duty harvesters**
   Today's logging is highly mechanised, and much of it is done by big machines called harvesters. These grab a tree, cut it with a chainsaw at the base, lower it to the ground, strip its branches and cut it into required lengths. A harvester can process three trees in a minute.

The Forestry Commission

Today the Forest of Dean is managed by Forestry England, part of the Forestry Commission. This organisation was created by the government when Britain was short of timber following World War I. It took over the Forest in 1924 but today, as well as timber, it has a strong focus on nature, environment, visitors and outdoor activities.

Coal

For hundreds of years, iron had been king in the Forest of Dean. But by the mid-1700s, miners were digging for coal instead of ore. Here is the story of how coal took over the throne and brought jobs for many, riches to a few and poverty to some.

Coal mining in the Forest

In the 1700s iron ore began to run out and so Freeminers turned to coal. There were about 150 small pits in the early 1800s: these were usually mines that tunnelled into a hillside. Flooding was a problem when going deeper. Permission to mine a gale (a plot of land) was granted by the Deputy Gaveller, and miners had to pay the crown for the right to dig and sell coal.

Big business

By the early 1800s many small pits were producing little coal, and Freeminers were too poor to buy winding gear and pumping equipment. This machinery was needed to reach the thicker seams of coal deeper down in the earth and to pump water out. The result was that many Freeminers sold their mines to outsiders or 'foreigners', as they were known. These rich businessmen made the mines bigger and deeper, providing more jobs. Soon over half the working men in the Forest were miners.

What is coal?

Coal is a soft black rock formed millions of years ago from dead trees and plants that were squashed under the weight of rocks building up on top of them. Coal is valuable because it can be burned as fuel.

The Forest rocks!

If you could slice down beneath the Forest with a giant knife you would see that it sits on a kind of saucer shape of different types of rock. On top of the old red sandstone is a bed of limestone and running through that are thin black layers (seams) of coal. In places they come to the surface but in the middle of the Forest they are deep underground.

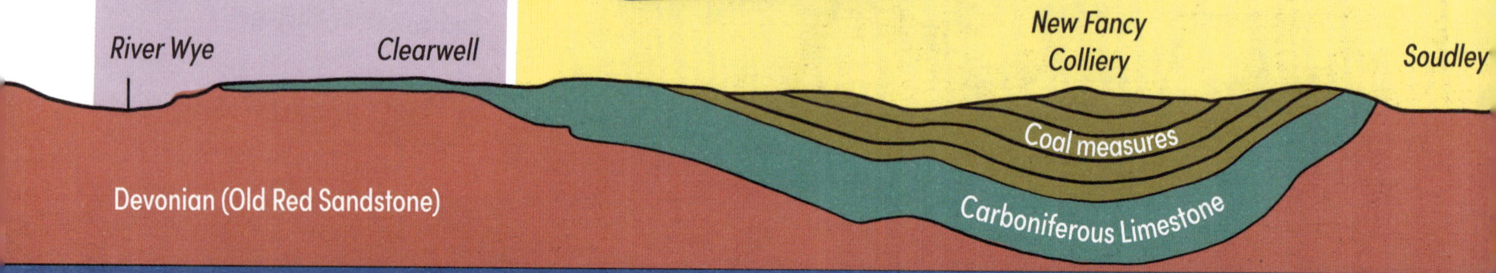

Crump Meadow Colliery, Near Cinderford. 1208.

River Wye | Clearwell | New Fancy Colliery | Soudley

Devonian (Old Red Sandstone) | Carboniferous Limestone | Coal measures

A collier's day

Digging coal was poorly paid and dangerous work. Many men were worn out by age 40. No wonder that miners sometimes went on strike!

★ Get up 5am
★ Walk to the pit
★ Hack away at coal with a pickaxe deep underground in the dark for hours
★ Short lunch break (often bread and cheese in a tommybag, plus cold tea)
★ Back to the coalface, working in cramped conditions
★ There were no toilets, so find a quiet corner in old workings
★ Walk home, often in the dark

Coalminer Charley Thomas, around 1940

In the cage

Here is how a pit owner's daughter described the journey down a mineshaft:

"The descent in the cage in the Forest pits was not achieved with the evenness of modern appliances. The sensation caused by the movement was akin to sea-sickness, the mental emotion almost weird. The shaft was narrow; the clay walls streamed with water; the slight board, which stood between you and the yawning depth below, shivered and bent under your feet. No relief was gained by an upward look; for every moment made the pit's mouth more distant until, at length, it was but a speck of light."
(Ada Trotter)

At the coalface, Lightmoor Colliery, 1930s

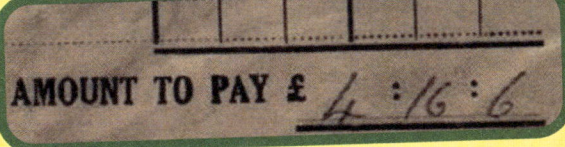
A miner's weekly payslip from 1944

Cage about to descend Trafalgar Colliery, near Cinderford.

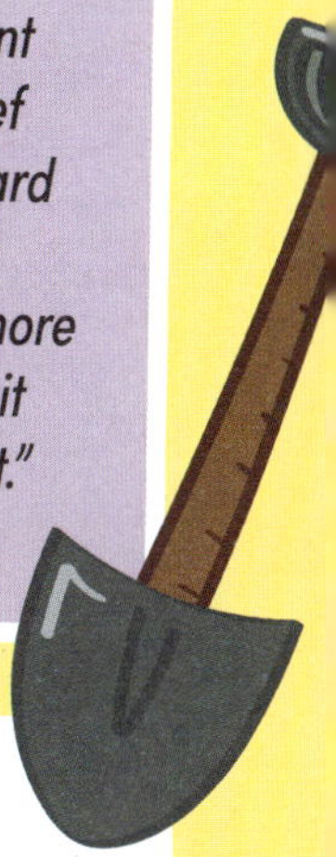

What coal was used for in Victorian times

Steam!

Demand for coal increased as the industrial revolution arrived in Britain and the age of machines took over. In the Forest, wealthy mine owners like the Crawshay family invested in steam engines to pump water out of the deep mines where flooding was a big problem. By 1898 Forest mines produced over one million tonnes of coal. It was taken by train and boat to big cities such as Bristol.

This steam engine was used at Lightmoor Colliery near Cinderford

Children in mines

Many coal mines were small family-owned pits, and boys and girls as young as six were expected to work in them. Small children could get into the low tunnels to carry out the coal. Many worked underground in the larger mines too: Bilson Colliery employed forty children under 13 in the 1840s. It was hard and dangerous work.

Hod boys

Boys as young as 9 and 10 dragged heavy carts of coal called hods from the coal face to the shaft. They crawled on hands and knees in dark tunnels often only 60cm high. Sharp stones cut them, and the leather strap fixed to the hod bit into their shoulders. Wages started at 3s (18p) a week for a 12-hour day, with only Sundays off.

There was no school for most Forest children until the late 1800s, so they were put to work

Carving of a Hod Boy in the Forest near Soudley

Banned?

Mine inspectors visited the Forest in 1841 and saw the horrific conditions that young children suffered. The result was a change in the law banning females and boys under 10 from working in mines.

Memories of former child miners. Another miner wrote: "The medicine for this soreness was to pee in a tin and, each day, dab the sore areas with one's own pee or 'body water' as it toughened up the skin." (Billy Cann)

Pit ponies at work

Pit ponies
Many ponies were used to haul heavy wagons of coal underground.

The decline of coal

By the early 1900s many older mines had closed as all of the coal was dug out. Costs rose sharply as mines went deeper (300m in places) and flooding increased. Eventually it became too expensive to mine coal in the Forest, and the last mine, Northern United, closed in 1965. Machinery was dismantled, shafts were blocked and huge spoil heaps were planted with trees. Slowly, the woodlands reclaimed the land.

Accidents and disasters

Coal mining has many different dangers. There were more than 600 deaths of miners recorded in the Forest, and when accidents happened rescue was difficult and treacherous. Hazards included:

★ Sudden flooding
★ Collapse of tunnels
★ Explosions (gunpowder was used to blast away rock)
★ Black damp: an invisible mixture of poisonous gases
★ Breathing in dust and stale air
★ Illness caused by lack of sunlight

The monument to the Union Pit disaster of 1902 when four men died in floods

| Coal output in the Forest of Dean ||
Year	Tonnes
1841	147,465
1860	599,945
1885	839,434
1900	1,066,850
1930	1,323,900
1950	734,600
1965	46,740

Coal mining today
There are still a few Freeminers working small pits in the Forest. One of these is at Hopewell Colliery, where visitors can go underground. It is well worth a trip.

The Union Pit rescue
Forest author Joyce Latham describes her uncle's memories of the disaster:

"The rescuers found three survivors out of the seven who had been entombed. Willing hands helped these weak, exhausted men on to stretchers, and bore them shoulder-high through the flood water and over rocks, timber and other debris, all in almost total darkness. It took them a long time to reach the cage at the shaft bottom, and Uncle Jim said he had never forgotten the patience and courage of those heroic miners. When at last they emerged into the September sunshine the anxious crowd burst spontaneously into a well-known hymn, 'Praise God From Whom All Blessings Flow'. It must have been a highly emotional moment, mixed equally with joy and anguish, and Uncle Jim was not too far-gone to notice seven coffins lined neatly at the pit-head, three of which remained empty."

A Freeminer in Monument Colliery using a compressed air jigger pick

Living in the forest

For centuries the Forest of Dean had no permanent inhabitants. The only people living among the woodlands were temporary residents: charcoal burners, along with officers of the king there to protect the trees and animals. Thousands of people live in the Forest today, so how did this change come about?

Lydbrook in the early 1900s. Many of these houses would have started out as small cabins.

Squatters

In the 1600s people who worked in the Forest, such as iron miners, charcoal makers and quarrymen, began to build small cabins around the edges of the royal land to live in. They made themselves gardens and orchards and kept animals such as goats, sheep and pigs. These people were known as squatters, and what they were doing was against the law.

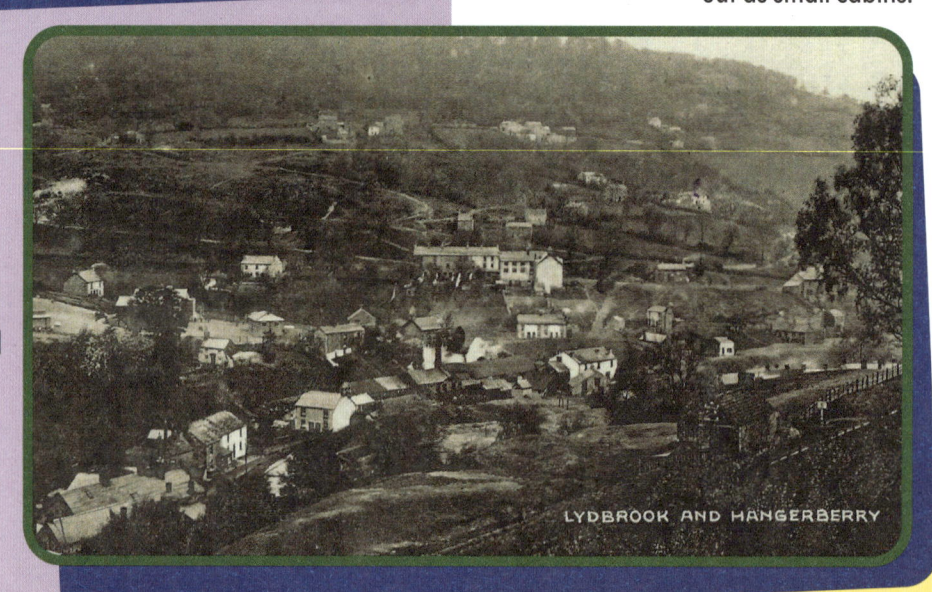

LYDBROOK AND HANGERBERRY

A charcoal maker's shelter

A squatter's cabin
These illegal homes were built with whatever was at hand: stones, wood and even mud. Roofs were made from turf or rushes and there were often no windows, although the cabins would have a fireplace and simple chimney. The cabins were small, damp and often filthy.

Scattered villages

By the 1750s the officers in charge of the Dean were putting up with squatters. Once more, cabins and cottages were built on the edges of Forest land by miners and others working locally. This was probably because their work brought money to the crown through rents and other payments. The encroachment continued into the 1800s, and villages became established, made up of small homes sprawled across the hillsides. There was no plan or control over building, which explains why so much of the Forest today is made up of higgledy-piggledy settlements.

Clear off!
By the 1660s the number of squatters living in the Forest illegally had increased. Many let their animals graze on nearby waste ground. Others stole wood for barrel-making or for fence posts. The authorities decided to clear all of them off crown land, and in 1662 they demolished 400 cabins and cottages.

Artwork by Helen Sandford

Cheeky!

Sometimes Foresters edged their fences and walls further into the Forest over time to gain more land. These encroachments even go on today, and boundaries are still checked by a Forestry England land surveyor.

Going legal

By 1838 there were so many people living in the Forest that the crown decided to make older homes legal. Recent squatters were offered the chance to buy the land they were living on. Many did, and built more solid two-storey stone homes. Some coalmine owners built terraced houses for their workers.

A miner's cottage

Most Forest miners lived in small two-bedroomed houses. Families in Victorian times and the early 1900s were usually large, and children might sleep 3-4 to a bed. The cottages often had a long strip of garden with a vegetable patch, chicken coop and a pigsty at the bottom.

A miner's clothes drying by the fire

Living without modern services

Many Foresters lived in houses they'd built themselves in the 1800s. Life was very different from today, and a typical family had none of these things:

★ Central heating
★ Drains
★ Piped water and taps
★ Bathrooms
★ Inside toilets
★ Electricity
★ Fridges, cookers and washing machines
★ Gas
★ TV
★ Definitely no Internet!

How would you manage without all of this?

A Forest childhood remembered

These drawings and memories are from Bernard Kear, who was a child growing up near Yorkley in the 1940s. His pictures and descriptions are collected in two wonderful books called Scenes of Childhood.

Toilets were outside in freezing cold sheds

"At night, images of terrible monsters prowling in the dark shadows of creaking sheds and water tanks haunted us when we needed the lavatory. For a small child it was terrifying ... inside the draught caused the candle flame to flicker, throwing sinister shadows onto walls ... we were scared that at any moment it would blow out."

Children often had to fetch water for washing and cooking

"The well was useful during sultry summers... we often lowered meat, milk and margarine into its chilly depths to prevent the hot weather from causing it to 'go off.'"

A town is born

Towns usually grow slowly over time and most of those in Britain are very old. Cinderford is different. The town didn't exist in Tudor times, but the building of a large ironworks in 1795 brought jobs and people. Coal mines such as Lightmoor, Foxes Bridge and Crump Meadow were also situated nearby, and during the 1800s lots of houses were built and the town grew very quickly. Cinderford soon became busy, as churches, schools, shops and inns were established.

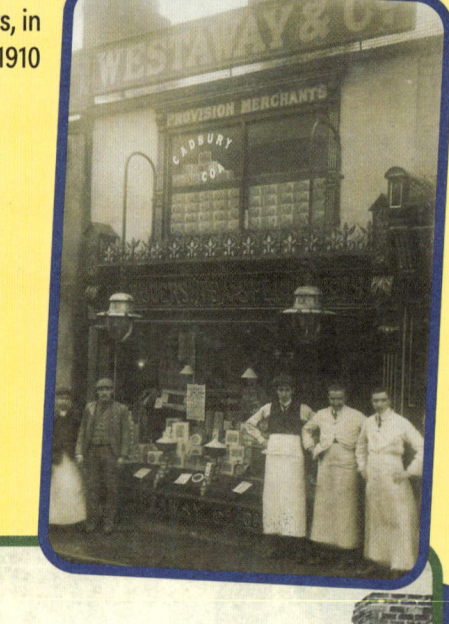

Westaway & Company, grocers, in Cinderford in 1910

Cinderford High Street in the early 1900s

Shop local!

People living in the Forest's towns and villages in the 1800s and early 1900s did their shopping locally. There were no cars or buses, and roads were poor for getting around by horse and cart or walking. Every village had several shops and inns, so people could usually buy what they wanted in their own community. Some Foresters never left the Forest in their lives!

In 1876 the village of Blakeney had the following shops and businesses:

- ★ 8 grocers
- ★ 5 drapers
- ★ 5 shoe and boot makers
- ★ 4 pubs
- ★ 2 butchers
- ★ 2 bakers
- ★ 2 dressmakers
- ★ A cooper
- ★ A blacksmith
- ★ A saddler
- ★ A hatmaker
- ★ A tailor
- ★ A chemist
- ★ A Post Office
- ★ A brewer
- ★ An ironmonger
- ★ A stationer
- ★ A watchmaker
- ★ Plus farmers, masons, plumbers, carpenters, millers, surgeons, and a police station!

A land without churches

Being royal land with no official inhabitants, for hundreds of years most of the Forest didn't have a church. As the population grew from 7,000 in 1831 to 27,000 in 1921, many chapels and churches were built. This helped to change the district:

★ Many Foresters became more respectable!
★ Some churches provided relief for the poor
★ Sunday schools enabled children to read and write
★ Churches often organised outings and entertainments (see page 51)

St Pauls in Parkend was one of the Forest's first new churches, opened in 1822

Commoning: Livestock in the Forest

The Forest of Dean has many ancient customs, and one of them is the tradition of local people letting their animals graze in the woods. This is sometimes called commoning. The medieval charter of 1217 allowed for pigs to forage in royal forests, and people later grazed cattle and ponies. At times, this led to disputes between the crown authorities and local people, with officials concerned that animals might destroy young trees.

Sheep badgers

Many miners and other Foresters were poor in the 1700s, and some kept a few sheep to provide food and income. This way of life soon spread, and by 1898 there were nearly 11,000 sheep roaming the Forest. A few local people, known as sheep badgers, continue this old custom today. There are now around 600 sheep which wander along the roads and through villages, often to the shock of visiting motorists!

The town donkey

In the past, commoners' cows and ponies used to wander round the Forest, including in the towns and villages. Cinderford even had a 'town donkey' roaming the streets in the 1940s. Its owner was fined after the donkey munched all the flowers in a local magistrate's garden!

Pigs traditionally fed on acorns and beech nuts in the woods: this is called pannage

Right or privilege?

There have been long arguments all through the history of the Forest, right up to the present day, about commoning animals here. Is it a right or a privilege (a kind of special favour)? What do you think?

41

Transport and travel

Travel through the steep, thickly wooded and industrial Forest has never been easy. Even today the roads are narrow and twist through the valleys and up the hills. Imagine how hard it was to move felled trees or wagons of heavy stone through the Forest in the past, before vehicles with engines were invented.

Barges could carry hundreds of tonnes of cargo in quite shallow water

Between two rivers

Over time the Forest has produced mountains of iron, coal, timber and stone, but how were these very heavy things moved to the distant places where they were needed? The answer is by river. For centuries the Forest's roads were just muddy tracks, useless for carting big loads. So before the railways arrived in the 1800s, trade moved along the two great rivers, the Severn and the Wye, on barges and sailing boats called trows.

Facts about the River Severn
- It flows through England and Wales for 220 miles (354km)
- It is Britain's longest river
- It has one of the highest tides in the world, rising and falling around 12m each day
- As well as fast tides it has dangerous mud, quicksand and strong currents
- The Severn bore is a famous wave caused by a very high tide being funnelled up the river

River ports
Coal, iron and other products were loaded onto boats at several busy ports along the Severn and Wye. These joined to canals, allowing goods to be transported long distances. Most of the trade went to Bristol and Gloucester, but some went to places as far as Ireland. The ports included:

- Lydney
- Newnham
- Lydbrook
- Redbrook

Getting across
Small ferry boats carried people and goods across the Severn for centuries. A railway bridge was opened in 1879, a railway tunnel in 1886 and finally a giant road bridge in 1966, enabling Foresters to drive to Bristol and beyond.

In 1960 two oil tankers collided with the railway bridge, destroying part of it, so that it later had to be dismantled. Five men died in the accident.

Lydney Harbour handled a lot of the Forest's coal in the 1800s

Tracks, trails and turnpikes

For thousands of years the Forest of Dean had no roads running through it. Instead, there were many ancient tracks and trails used by miners, ironworkers and charcoal burners. When roads were made, they were steep, muddy and full of deep ruts. One traveller of 1721 described them as "impassable".

A Forest tramway: sometimes ropes were used to haul the wagons up hills

The toll house between Parkend and Coleford is still there today (shown here in 1888). The road on the left goes to Bream.

Tramroads

Until the late 1700s most of the coal and iron produced by the Forest had to be moved by packhorse. It was too heavy to be carted along the Forest's steep hills and poor roads. But as outside owners took over the mines, they paid for tramroads to be built. These were narrow railways along which strong horses pulled wagons called drams to docks on the Severn and Wye.

Turnpikes and tolls
In the late 1700s a turnpike trust controlled the Forest's roads. Toll gates were put up and travellers had to pay to use the roads, with the money going towards building and repairs.

Trains take over

In the 1800s a new technology was developed which could haul huge amounts of heavy coal: the steam train. The Forest's first railway was opened in 1854 to carry goods. New lines were added in the following years, with tunnels blasted under hills to connect coalmines. Stations were built, and the first passenger service was opened in 1875. This joined the main line to Gloucester and Wales, enabling Foresters to travel to places they'd never seen before.

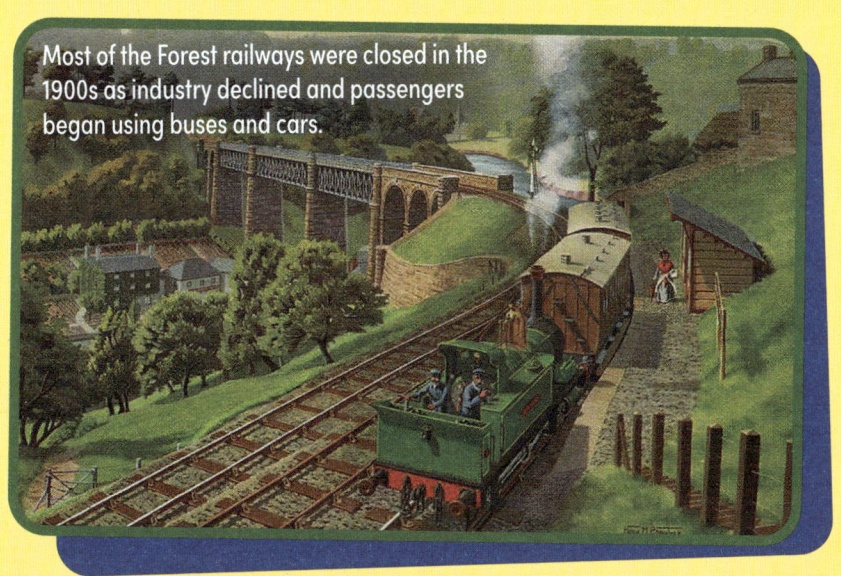

Most of the Forest railways were closed in the 1900s as industry declined and passengers began using buses and cars.

This map shows how railways connected the Forest's mines in 1880

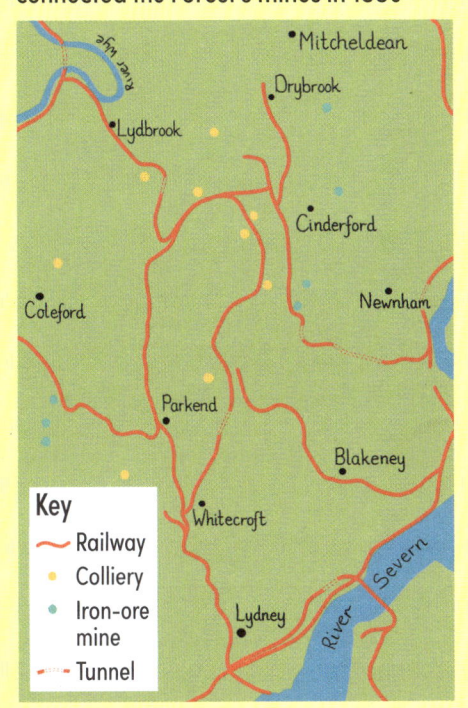

Key
- Railway
- Colliery
- Iron-ore mine
- Tunnel

The Dean Forest Railway
Steam engines still pull trains today on the old Severn and Wye heritage route between Lydney and Parkend.

Dean Forest Railway
THE FRIENDLY FOREST LINE

43

Poverty

The history of the Forest of Dean reveals many times when ordinary people had little money and struggled to manage their lives. Support from government, such as benefits, didn't exist until very recently, and many families had to rely on charity. Not everyone was poor, of course, but for many, daily life was hard in all kinds of ways.

The Freeminers struggle

In the late 1700s many mining families in the Forest were poor. Freeminers often struggled to make enough money for food, and some couldn't afford to pay the rents on their mines. Others needed machinery to reach deep coal and tackle flooding but had no money to buy it. These miners often lived in primitive cabins in filthy conditions.

Riots again

There were bread riots in the Forest in 1795 and 1801 as people ran out of food. Poverty was one of the causes of later riots too, as the crown enclosed much of the Forest, preventing many local people from grazing the animals they depended on.

Changes in the 1800s

Businessmen from outside the Forest bought collieries and paid for pumping equipment, which led to an increase in jobs as mines could go deeper and reach thicker seams of coal. But this meant that most Forest miners were no longer their own bosses. They were employed by the owners who often paid them low wages and expected long 12-hour working days in return.

A grim home life?

Things in the early 1800s were hard at home as well as at work for a lot of Forest miners. More jobs meant more people needing places to live. Towns such as Cinderford were overcrowded and had open drains with sewage running between houses.

Twin fears: Unemployment and the workhouse

In some years the price of coal fell, and miners found themselves out of work. Sometimes wages were cut and miners went on strike, unable to feed their families. People feared the shame of being sent to the dreaded workhouse, where they would have to work for basic food and bed in miserable conditions. A few Foresters chose to emigrate and look for a new life abroad at this time.

Shocking numbers

41
The average lifespan of people in 1841 in England (today it is over 80)

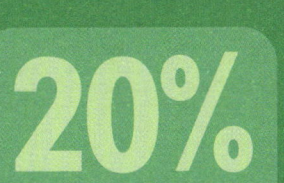

20%
The ratio of babies that died in the 1800s (this was higher in very poor families)

6
The average number of children in a Victorian family (many had over 10)

42p
The daily pay of a typical Forest miner in 1921 (this is roughly equal to £17 today)

The 1926 strike

The year 1926 was a cruel time for the 6,500 miners in the Forest of Dean. The mine owners were facing high costs, mainly due to bad flooding in the pits. They planned to cut the wages of miners by a quarter. The miners knew that many people couldn't live on this. They called a union meeting and voted to strike, meaning that they refused to work for the lower wage. The strike lasted 33 weeks and caused much suffering as families went hungry. In the end, the miners were defeated and had to work for less pay, with many also losing their jobs.

Mounted police were called in to break up fights between striking miners and those who wanted to return to work.

Winifred Foley

Winifred was the daughter of a Forest miner. She wrote a wonderful book called *A Child in the Forest*, telling the story of growing up in the early 1900s. You can find out more about her on page 55.

Here are some of Winifred's memories of the 1920s:

> We were never anything but poor ... the dirt brought home from the pit, and on our boots, fought a constant battle with Mam's determination not to have her house 'turned into a turnpike road'.

> Candles and paraffin lamps lit us up... often our home couldn't afford paraffin – or even, on occasion, a candle.

> ...our water, apart from the rainwater, caught from the roof in tubs, came from a well a quarter of a mile away ...

> The village had no drains and no dustmen.

> Privy buckets were emptied into holes dug in the garden.

> Life was wonderful except for one constant nagging irritation: hunger.

> ... the back bedroom, three to a bed.

The Forest at war

The early tribes that inhabited the Forest often fought each other, and in later times Freeminers were called up to help medieval kings win their battles. There are three wars that deeply affected the Forest, however, and led to the tragic loss of many brave men and women. The last of these is within living memory.

The English Civil War

In 1642 a very bloody war broke out between the king and parliament. King Charles I's supporters were called Royalists and they included Sir John Winter, the owner of several ironworks in the Forest. Winter was unpopular because he enclosed large parts of the woodland that Foresters used to graze their animals. He used his forges to make cannons, cannonballs and other weapons, although he had to flee when parliament won the war.

The Battle of Coleford

The Civil War came to the Forest in 1643 when an army of 2,000 Welsh Royalists laid siege to Coleford, which was defended by a much smaller force of mainly local people fighting for parliament. The Foresters shot at the invaders from houses but had to run into the Forest and hide in the mines to avoid being killed.

Members of the Sealed Knot re-enacting the battle in Coleford in 2018

World War I

Many Forest men joined the armed forces during World War I and several were killed. Their names are recorded on war memorials in the towns and villages. A number of memorial halls were built after the war, like this one at Whitecroft, to remember those who bravely fought for their country.

Three local heroes of WWI

Who was he?
FW Harvey was a poet and local solicitor who lived in Yorkley for many years.

What did he do?
He was awarded the Distinguished Conduct Medal for capturing an enemy listening post in France in 1915. He was later captured by the Germans and became a prisoner of war.

Who was he?
Angus Buchanan from Coleford joined the army from university.

What did he do?
He was awarded the Victoria Cross (the highest military honour) for rescuing two wounded men under fire. He was later blinded when shot by a sniper.

Who was he?
Francis Miles was a miner from Clearwell who enlisted in the army aged just 18.

What did he do?
He was awarded the Victoria Cross for capturing two dangerous machine gun posts single handed. He returned home to a hero's welcome.

World War II

The Forest was important in World War II because its coal helped to produce the power needed to make vehicles and weapons, while its timber had many uses. It was also a quiet base for US troops and somewhere safe to store ammunition. It had other roles too, outlined here:

The secret factory
Pine End Works near Lydney was built during the war to make plywood for the famous Mosquito bomber and other wooden aircraft. Workers were not allowed to talk about their work there in case the Germans found out and bombed the factory.

The Mosquito was one of the fastest planes used in WWII

Prisoners in the Forest
Here are five facts about local PoWs (prisoners of war):

1. A number of captured Italian and German soldiers were held in a PoW camp near Coleford during the 1940s
2. Some were let out of the camp to work locally
3. Many of the prisoners made friends with Foresters and their families
4. Some of the PoWs used their work skills to make gifts for local people
5. A group of the Italians formed a football team that was allowed to play in a local league!

Lumberjills
Around 400 women became emergency forestry workers in the Forest during the war, to replace men called up to fight. The Women's Timber Corps, known as lumberjills (a female version of lumberjacks), did vital work to supply wood for the war effort.

Memorial hunt
? Does your town or village have a war memorial?
? Can you find it?
? Do you recognise any of the surnames listed?
? Which wars does it mention?

The Italian prisoners' team in the 1940s

Crime and punishment

For a beautiful area of quiet woodland, the Forest of Dean has witnessed a surprisingly large amount of crime in the last thousand years. Trees offer cover and the chance to hide and sneak about, and perhaps carry away timber or animals. Some people even 'stole' the land itself to build on, and when the authorities fought back there were many clashes involving angry mobs and a series of riots. It was not always quiet!

Poaching

Trapping, killing or taking animals from the Forest without permission is something that has gone on for centuries. Poaching has always been against the law, but for many poor Foresters the temptation was too great. A deer or boar could feed a hungry family for weeks and so poachers often fought battles with the gamekeepers and officers who tried to stop them, with much blood spilled.

Naughty officials

In the Middle Ages and later, a lot of the officers in charge of the Forest were dishonest. In return for bribes (usually money), they turned a blind eye to a great deal of poaching, timber stealing and unlawful building on royal land.

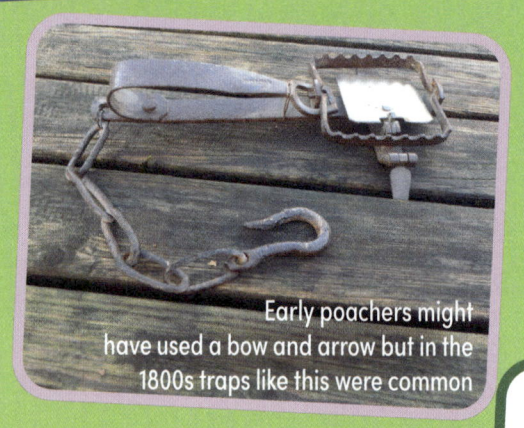

Early poachers might have used a bow and arrow but in the 1800s traps like this were common

Rustlers!

Sheep stealing was common in the 1700s and 1800s, with cattle and horses also being targeted. The risk of being caught was severe, however: offenders could be hanged.

Death and dynamite!

In 1895 a policeman was killed with a stone thrown by a local man at Viney Hill. Three years later a steam-powered sawing machine near Blakeney was blown up using dynamite. The machine was being used to make fences for inclosures. The same night over 50 small fires were started in the Forest nearby. The Deputy Surveyor, Philip Baylis, announced that this was sure to be the work of the 'Blakeney Gang', a band of local criminals known for poaching and sheep stealing. But others argued that the authorities were using these incidents as an excuse to fence off large parts of the Forest and so stop local people from grazing their animals. The later crimes remained unsolved.

£100 REWARD.

Whereas on the night of the 9th of February, 1898, some person or persons did feloniously wreck, by DYNAMITE, near Blakeney Hill, in the Forest of Dean, a STEAM SAWING MACHINE

This is to give Notice that the above Reward will be paid by the undersigned to any person who shall give such information as will lead to the Arrest and Conviction of the Offender or Offenders.

HENRY CHRISTIAN,
Chief Constable of Gloucestershire.
Chief Constable's Office,
Cheltenham, March 7th, 1898.

A huge reward was offered for information about the dynamite crime: £100 was more than a miner would earn in a whole year

The Forest of Dean Verderers still meet in the Court Room at Speech House

Punishments

A court met in the Forest in medieval times to deal with offenders. The Normans sometimes cut off two of a poacher's fingers for killing one of the king's deer. In later times, most punishments involved fines or jail terms, but murderers were hanged and some offenders were whipped.

A newspaper cutting from the early 1900s

★★★
Littledean Police Court: George Brain, James Brain, and William Church, youths, were summoned for playing pitch and toss on Sunday evening last at Bilston Green. Pc white proved the case. The defendants were let off on paying costs and ordered to come up for judgement when called.

The Story of Warren James and the 1831 Riots

Artwork by Helen Sandford

The Forest was in a poor state in the year 1808. Many squatters were living in rough cabins, huge numbers of sheep roamed freely, and there were very few trees left for shipbuilding.

That year a man called Edward Machen became Deputy Surveyor, in charge of the Forest. He took action and began to build walls and fences around 4,452 hectares (11,000 acres) and plant oaks for the navy. These inclosures protected the young trees from being eaten by sheep and deer.

Machen's actions caused a lot of anger among local people, especially the Freeminers. Many of them were poor and the inclosures stopped them grazing their animals and collecting wood. Once the young trees had grown, the Foresters expected the fences to be taken down.

In 1831 one of the miners, Warren James, called for the inclosures to be opened up. When Machen refused after talks, James led a large crowd of miners and other local people to tear down the inclosures around Parkend.

Machen sent for troops, and a force of armed soldiers stopped the riots, which by this time had involved over a thousand people. Warren James was arrested as the leader of the rebels and sentenced to death.

Later, the sentence was changed and James was instead transported on a convict ship to Van Diemen's Land (Tasmania, near Australia) where he died 10 years later. Today, some people think of Warren James as a folk hero for standing up for the rights of Foresters.

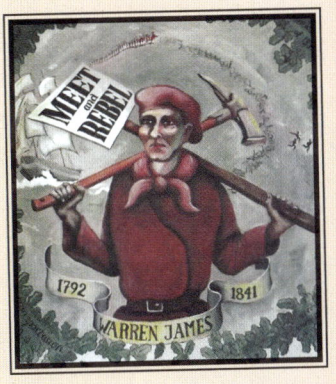

A mural by Tom Cousins, in the Fountain Inn, Parkend

49

Other industries

As well as coal mining, iron making and forestry, other jobs have been notable in the history of the Dean.

Fishermen at Purton with a lave net and salmon, around 1930

Quarrying

Local stone has long been used for building and paving and to make lime for cement. There are many small disused quarries across the Forest, and for centuries many men were employed blasting, cutting and moving blocks of red and grey sandstone and limestone. Some quarrying and stone cutting still goes on today.

Fetter Hill Quarry near Coleford in 1908

Fishing

People from the Forest have always fished in the Severn and Wye, especially for the big salmon that once swam up the rivers in large numbers. Various kinds of nets and traps were used.

Putchers are baskets used to catch large fish

Other industries

Here are just a few of the many jobs that Foresters have done over time:

- **Boat building:** Barges and larger ships were built at ports along the Severn and Wye
- **Sawmills:** In these, local timber was cut into posts, boards and more to sell on
- **Chemical works:** Factories, where substances like acid, tar and alcohol were made from wood
- **Tinplating:** There were tinplate works at Lydney and Lydbrook that produced thin sheets of metal for all kinds of uses
- **Engineering:** Several workshops sprang up to make parts for coal mines and for the steam engines that pumped water out of them
- **Rank Xerox:** This large company employed 5,000 people in Mitcheldean in the 1960s, making copiers and office equipment

Thirsty work
These two famous drinks are made at the Suntory plant in Coleford at the rate of five bottles a second!

Gold in the hills?

In 1906 there was much excitement in the Forest when a gold mine was established at Lea Bailey, near Mitcheldean. Traces of the precious metal had been found in some of the rocks. Many people bought £1 shares in the mine (equal to more than £100 today) hoping to get rich, but lost their money when two years of digging produced almost nothing.

Entertainment and community events

In the past, most people had to make their own entertainment and there were many ways of doing this. Shared community events were very popular and often involved dressing up, as you can see from these old photographs.

Popular sports in the Forest included rugby, football and cricket: this is Ruspidge United football team in 1953

Pillowell Silver Band in 1947

Special days

Before the invention of television and the Internet, families looked forward to special events to provide fun and entertainment. These often took place in summer and included:

- ★ Church outings
- ★ Carnivals
- ★ Parades
- ★ Fairs
- ★ Coach trips to the seaside

Fancy dress at Cinderford Carnival around 1953

Music and singing

Many of the Forest's collieries had their own bands, and there was strong competition between silver or brass bands, with regular contests to win trophies. Singing was also popular, and many villages and towns had their own choirs. Some of these bands and choirs are still going today.

Children's games

Forest children spent much of their time playing in the woods. Popular things to do included:

- ★ Climbing trees
- ★ Making dens
- ★ Chasing games
- ★ Rope swings
- ★ Shooting catapults
- ★ Jumping into the bracken (ferns)
- ★ Damming streams
- ★ Playing 'cowboys and Indians'
- ★ Conkers
- ★ Exploring ash tips and old quarries

Childhood memories of the 1920s

The highlight of the year would be the 'Sunday School Treat'. We would make our way from the Chapel to Whitecroft station and on to the pleasure gardens at Sharpness with a bunch of sweet Peas in my lapel and tuppence in my pocket.

The Miners' outing was another day that families looked forward to with a day at the sea-side. On one of these outings I can recall going to Blackpool for the day by train for 4/6d return (22.5p).

Our hours of leisure after school in the light evenings was spent running with a hoop and the handle of a galvanized bucket up through Clements End Green and Sling and back down Bream Avenue.

Schools and education

Before the late 1800s, most children in the Forest didn't go to school and as a result, many Foresters were unable to read and write. What was life like for children when the first schools were built?

New schools

Before 1870, education was mostly for the rich, but that year the government passed a law ruling that all children aged 5–10 must attend school. Soon, lots of new primary schools were built around the Forest in places such as Littledean, Broadwell, Drybrook and English Bicknor, and many of these are still in use today. Most children left school aged 12 in the 1800s and then went to work, although this changed after the first secondary school was opened in Cinderford in 1896.

A Victorian school day
★ The day lasted from 9 am until 5 pm
★ School was strict, dull and uncomfortable
★ Most lessons involved repetitive English and maths exercises
★ Everyone was expected to work in silence
★ Discipline was harsh: unruly pupils were slapped with rulers, or caned

Viney Hill School in 1916, 1948 and 1965: what changes do you notice?

Busy schools

Many of the new Forest schools were overcrowded, with large classes. Look at these surprising numbers:

Year	School	Total pupils
1889	Steam Mills	241
1904	Pillowell	505
1910	Soudley	167
1910	Yorkley	259
1910	Ellwood	279
1910	Ruardean Woodside	311

HOOF

Hands off our Forest

Three times, in 1981, 1993 and 2010, the government has tried to sell the country's publicly owned forests, including the Forest of Dean. Many local people felt very strongly that this was wrong, and so in 2010 they formed a campaign group called Hands Off Our Forest (HOOF).

The Forest in danger?

The Forest of Dean is owned by the nation and run by a government organisation called Forestry England. But in 2010 politicians began to discuss the idea of possibly selling the Forest to other organisations. This caused a lot of anger and worry among Foresters. Their fears included:

★ Not being free to walk and cycle around all parts of the Forest
★ A possible increase in building or industry
★ The loss of woodland
★ Damage to wildlife

A rally in the snow

A public meeting was called in January 2011 and more than 1,000 people turned up at Speech House meadow during a fall of snow to hear speakers talk about the importance of saving the Forest.

Success!

The HOOF campaign gathered a lot of support, and the government dropped its plans to sell off the Forest, although some people believe that it could happen in the future.

Murals on the houses of HOOF supporters in Coalway, painted by Tom Cousins

Get involved

Between 2017 and 2022, a programme called Foresters' Forest has run projects and events with community groups, supported by the National Lottery Heritage Fund. These have helped people become aware of everything that makes the Forest of Dean special, and enabled Foresters to get involved with looking after it in the future.

FORESTERS' FOREST

HERITAGE FUND

What do you think?
★ Should the Forest be owned by everybody?
★ Should it be run by a charity?
★ Should it be protected?

Tourism

For centuries, very few outsiders visited the Forest of Dean. For many people outside the district, it was a wild, unknown place, populated by rough miners and fierce people living in huts among the woods. But today the Forest is full of visitors, and tourism is important for local businesses.

Train trips
Visitors began to explore the Forest in the late 1800s when the railways were open. An illustrated tourist guide was published in 1880 for the price of 6d (2½p).

A National Forest Park
As the coal industry declined in the 1900s, tourism was promoted in the hope it would create local jobs. In 1938 the Forest became the UK's first National Forest Park, and campsites were opened to attract visitors. Unfortunately, World War II began the following year!

Attractions

Puzzlewood was created in the 1920s, allowing people to explore the ancient scowles near Milkwall. Several more visitor attractions followed in the years afterwards:

- The Dean Forest Railway
- The Forest of Dean Sculpture Trail
- Ponds, lakes and picnic areas such as Mallards Pike
- Clearwell Caves
- Symonds Yat Rock viewpoint
- Canoe hire on the River Wye
- The Dean Heritage Centre
- Hopewell Colliery visitor centre
- The family cycle trail

Several of these have been created on the sites of mines and other Forest industries.

Getting active
Today, many people come to the Forest to enjoy outdoor activities such as walking, mountain biking, caving and canoeing.

The Forest has lots of exciting mountain bike trails to attract riders

The Cathedral sculpture

Notable people

Several people who grew up in and around the Forest have gone on to lead interesting lives. Here are details of a few of them:

Winifred Foley (1914-2009)

★ Born in Brierley in a mining family
★ Left home aged 14 to work as a servant in a house in London
★ Became a writer when she sent her memories of growing up in the Forest to the BBC, who made them into a radio serial.
★ Her true stories were published in a popular book called *A Child in the Forest*

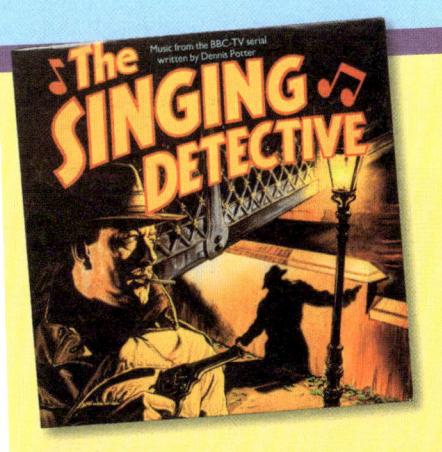

Dennis Potter (1935-1994)

★ Born in Berry Hill
★ A writer, most famous for creating several classic TV dramas.
★ His best-known plays include:
  ▶ *Pennies from Heaven* (1978)
  ▶ *Blue Remembered Hills* (1979), set in the Forest of Dean
  ▶ *The Singing Detective* (1986)
★ A whole gallery of the Dean Heritage Centre is devoted to his life

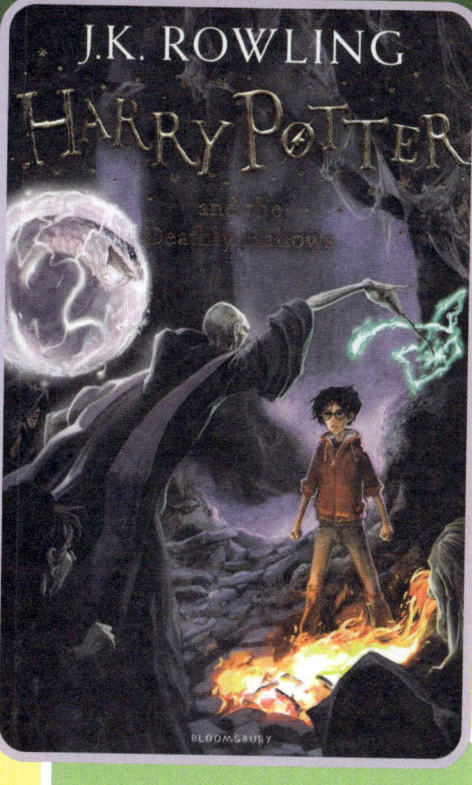

JK Rowling (born 1965)

★ Lived in Tutshill, near Chepstow, from the age of 9 until leaving home at 18
★ World famous for the Harry Potter fantasy stories, the highest-selling book series of all time
★ The Forest of Dean features in the final book of the series, *Harry Potter and the Deathly Hallows*

Who else lived in the Forest?

Herbert Howells: Composer of church music, from Lydney

FW Harvey: Poet, famous for the poem *Ducks*, who lived at Yorkley

Jimmy Young: BBC radio DJ, from Cinderford

Steve James: Former England cricketer, from Lydney

Some of the Forest's best writers are celebrated in murals like this one in Coleford, made by Tom Cousins

Places to visit

Here are some places which help to bring alive the history of the Forest:

Dean Heritage Centre

Where is it? Soudley
What is it? An excellent museum and visitor centre with outdoor and indoor exhibits
What can you see? Galleries about the history of the Forest, a Victorian schoolroom, a forester's cottage, a charcoal burner's camp and more
What can you do? Explore the grounds, try out the interactive displays and join in special events

Hopewell Colliery Museum

Where is it? Near Coleford
What is it? A real working coal mine run by Freeminer and Verderer Rich Daniels
What can you see? What the Forest is like below ground, and a coal seam with workings
What can you do? Wear a helmet and miner's lamp, enjoy a guided tour and discover the cramped, dark conditions that colliers once worked in (and still do today!)

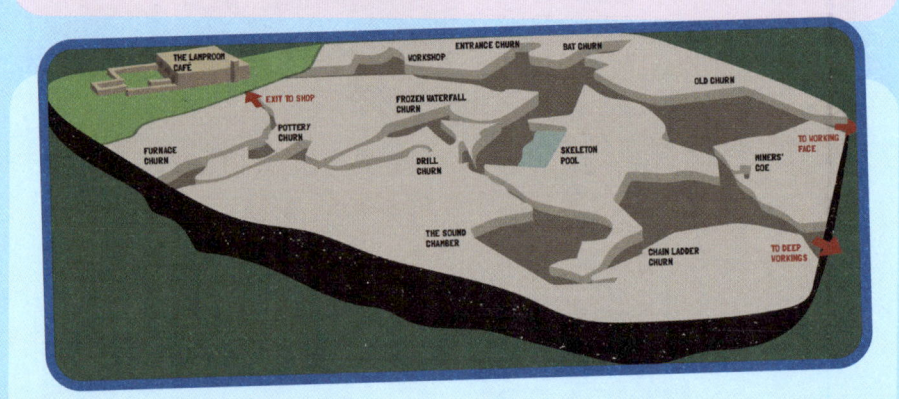

Clearwell Caves

Where is it? Near Clearwell
What is it? A group of ancient iron mines you can explore
What can you see? The well-lit caverns are full of surprises and interesting displays
What can you do? Go underground and discover what life was like as an iron miner; nearby is the Secret Forest with a reconstruction of an Iron Age village

Dean Forest Railway

Where is it? Lydney to Parkend
What is it? A steam engine ride through the Forest
What can you see? Old locomotives and carriages, restored stations, smoke and steam!
What can you do? Find out what train travel through the Forest used to be like on the route of the old Severn and Wye Railway

Other interesting places

★ **Puzzlewood**: A memorable walk through the ancient iron workings and caves called scowles
★ **St Briavels Castle**: The original headquarters of the Forest as a royal hunting ground for kings
★ **Symonds Yat**: The famous viewpoint over the Wye that was once an Iron Age fort
★ **Lydney Harbour**: Where much of the Forest's coal, iron and timber was shipped out
★ **Speech House**: The Forest's former courtroom and HQ, now a hotel with tearoom
★ **Lydney Park**: The location of a Roman temple high up on a hill
★ **New Fancy Geomap**: A giant map of Forest mines on the site of an old colliery
★ **Darkhill Ironworks**: The site of secret experiments to make the best steel possible

Forest Dialect

In the past, Forest people used all kinds of words and phrases that are special to the area. This is known as dialect. Here is a collection of Forest words from Bernard Kear's *Scenes of Childhood* books:

Expression	Meaning
bellock	shout
brevetting	wandering about
browst	twigs
butty	friend
comp	candle
coochy	snuggle
daddecky	partly rotten
daggled	exhausted
dappy	bouncy
dree	three
dussunt	do not
gyule	sneer
hommocks	legs
jadder	liar
mokey	donkey
nern	none
oot	will you
spitter	spade
tush	pull
vire	fire
watty-handed	clumsy
wiffle	stink
wum	home
yud	head

Patter puzzle

Can you work out what this means?

"Thee'st needn't gyule, thee duss knaw I was vust."

Image credits

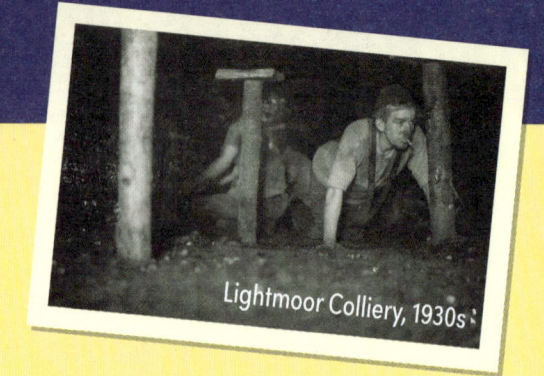

Lightmoor Colliery, 1930s

Clearwell Caves

Page 1: New Venture free mine, Nick Hodgson; **Page 1:** Acorn and oak leaf, Valzan/Shutterstock.com; **Page 2:** Ruspidge-United 1952-53, JackieSannwald; **Page 2:** Charcoal loading, Forestry England; **Page 3:** Roman soldier, Ionuticlanzan/Shutterstock.com; **Page 3:** Yorkley Coins, Dean Heritage Centre; **Page 3:** Sheep, Eric Isselee/Shutterstock.com; **Page 3:** Cave hyena, Matyas/Shutterstock.com; **Page 3:** Mosquito aircraft in flight, BlueBarronPhoto/Shutterstock.com; **Page 3:** £100 Reward poster, Ian Wright; **Page 3:** Hopewell Colliery, John French; **Page 3:** HOOF leaf logo, Viv Hargreaves; **Page 3:** Medieval boar, Andy Seed; **Page 3:** Fallow deer, Ekaterina V. Borisova/Shutterstock.com; **Page 3:** Iron Age coin, Dean Archaeological Group; **Page 4:** Freeminers crest, © Clearwell Caves; **Page 4:** Medieval deer hunt, Livre de La Chasse by Gaston Phoebus. Public domain, via Wikimedia Commons; **Page 4:** Miners in cage, Ian Pope; **Page 5:** Romans fighting celts, Massimo Todaro/Shutterstock.com; **Page 5:** Bronze Age sword, iStock.com/Norbert_Speicher; **Page 5:** Viney Hill School 1948, Rosemary Cleworth; **Page 5:** Miners, Rich Daniels; **Page 5:** Yorkley Coins, Dean Heritage Centre; **Page 5:** Dean Forest Mercury , John Powell; **Page 5:** Flint arrowhead, Dean Heritage Centre; **Page 5:** Lumberjills , Ruth Fletcher; **Page 6:** Big map of Forest, Ursula Hurst; **Page 8:** Hunter-gathers, ©Worcestershire County Council; **Page 8:** Wolf, Jim Cumming/Shutterstock.com; **Page 8:** Arrowhead, Dean Heritage Centre; **Page 8:** Bronze Age people/homes, © Look and Learn; **Page 8:** Bronze Age sword, iStock.com/Norbert_Speicher; **Page 8:** Trees background art, Pogorelova Olga/Shutterstock.com; **Page 9:** Iron Age settlement, © Look and Learn; **Page 9:** Axe, Public domain via Look and Learn and The Metropolitan Museum of Art; **Page 9:** Hook, Public domain via Look and Learn and The Metropolitan Museum of Art; **Page 9:** Blade, Public domain via Look and Learn and The Metropolitan Museum of Art; **Page 9:** Hill fort, Hillfort reconstruction illustration by Phil Kenning of Kenning Illustration Ltd; **Page 9:** Iron Age coin, Dean Archaeological Group; **Page 10:** Romano-British people, ©Worcestershire County Council; **Page 10:** Roman soldier, Ionuticlanzan/Shutterstock.com; **Page 10:** Lydney Temple remains, Clive Mann/Creative Commons; **Page 10:** Lydney Dog, Courtesy Chris Sullivan; **Page 11:** Anglo-Saxon village, © Look and Learn; **Page 11:** Athelstan , © Look and Learn; **Page 11:** Offa's Dyke photo, ARG_Flickr/Creative Commons; **Page 12:** Norman people, © Look and Learn; **Page 12:** Red deer, Eric Isselee/Shutterstock.com; **Page 12:** William I, © Look and Learn; **Page 12:** St Briavels Castle, Andy Seed; **Page 13:** Knight in armour, Rorius/Shutterstock.com; **Page 13:** Henry III, © Look and Learn; **Page 13:** Freeminers crest, © Clearwell Caves; **Page 14:** Black death, Unknown author, Public domain, via Wikimedia Commons; **Page 14:** Medieval axe head, Dean Heritage Centre; **Page 14:** Medieval village, ©Worcestershire County Council; **Page 15:** Tudor miner, Andy Seed; **Page 15:** Henry VIII, National Portrait Gallery, Public domain, via Wikimedia Commons; **Page 15:** Elizabeth I, National Portrait Gallery, Public domain, via Wikimedia Commons; **Page 15:** Walter Raleigh, National Portrait Gallery, Public domain, via Wikimedia Commons; **Page 15:** Golden Hinde, © Look and Learn; **Page 15:** Blast furnace, Alison Whitby and the Lake District National Park Authority; **Page 15:** Tudor Document, National Archives; **Page 15:** Tudor chair, iStock.com/Peter Llewellyn; **Page 16:** Poor people, Historical Images Archive / Alamy Stock Photo; **Page 16:** Charles I, Follower of Anthony van Dyck, Public domain, via Wikimedia Commons; **Page 16:** Civil War soldier, © Look and Learn; **Page 17:** Public notice, Ian Wright; **Page 18:** Mining family, Ian Pope; **Page 18:** Row of houses, Ian Pope; **Page 18:** Child miner , National Coal Mining Museum for England; **Page 18:** Fallow deer, Ekaterina V. Borisova/Shutterstock.com; **Page 19:** Severn Rail Bridge, Dean Heritage Centre; **Page 19:** Dancing bear, Personal correspondence, Public domain, via Wikimedia Commons; **Page 19:** Foxes Bridge Colliery, Dean Heritage Centre; **Page 19:** Dean Forest Mercury , John Powell; **Page 20:** Downham family, Maureen Byrne; **Page 20:** War memorial, Eric Nicholls; **Page 20:** Dennis Potter, Geraint Lewis / Alamy Stock Photo; **Page 21:** Cable works, Terry Burton; **Page 21:** hooter, anonymous contributor; **Page 21:** JK Rowling, Featureflash Photo Agency/Shutterstock.com; **Page 21:** Giant chair, John French; **Page 22:** Early people round fire, Ursula Hurst; **Page 22:** Cave hyena, Matyas/Shutterstock.com; **Page 23:** Iron age fort Symonds Yat, Wye Valley AONB; **Page 23:** Roman soldiers, Massimo Todaro/Shutterstock.com; **Page 23:** Yorkley Coins, Dean Heritage Centre; **Page 24:** Medieval deer hunt, Livre de La Chasse by Gaston Phoebus. Public domain, via Wikimedia Commons; **Page 24:** Boar spit roast, Public domain image; **Page 24:** Forest boundary map, Ursula Hurst;

Freemining today

Forestry horses at work

Page 25: St Briavels Castle photo, © Historic England Photo Library;
Page 25: Roe Deer, Eric Isselee/Shutterstock.com; **Page 25:** Boar illustration, Andy Seed; **Page 25:** Boar photo, Forestry England; **Page 25:** Verderers, Sue Middleton;
Page 26: Iron and coal map, Ursula Hurst; **Page 27:** Elaine Morman, Phillipa Klaiber and Elaine Morman; **Page 27:** Medieval crossbow & bolts, CallumFTW/Shutterstock.com; **Page 28:** Iron ore, James St. John (Creative Commons); **Page 28:** Bloomery furnace diagram, Ursula Hurst; **Page 28:** Blast furnace diagram, Ursula Hurst;
Page 28: Whitecliff ironworks, Cheryl Mayo; **Page 29:** James I, after John de Critz (died 1641), Public domain, via Wikimedia Commons; **Page 29:** Robert Mushet, Dean Heritage Centre; **Page 29:** ochre, ErickN/Shutterstock.com; **Page 30:** Charter of the Forest, © The British Library Board; **Page 30:** Charcoal making photos, Mark Ward;
Page 31: Medieval tanner, © Look and Learn; **Page 31:** Ships v Iron cartoon, Ursula Hurst; **Page 31:** Photo of HMS Victo**Page 31:** Painting of Nelson, Greenwich Hospital Collection; **Page 32:** Woodcut of Warren James, Clifford Harper; **Page 32:** Freemine, Rich Daniels; **Page 32:** Enclosure wall, Martin Latham;
Page 33: Langdale axe, Dean Heritage Centre; **Page 33:** Crosscut sawing, Forestry England; **Page 33:** Harvester, Forestry Commission; **Page 33:** Horse logging, Forestry England; **Page 33:** Forestry England logo, Forestry England; **Page 34:** Crump Meadow Colliery, Dean Heritage Centre; **Page 34:** Geology of Forest, Gloucestershire Geological Trust; **Page 35:** Coalminer Charley Thomas, Dean Heritage Centre;
Page 35: At the coalface Lightmoor, Rich Daniels; **Page 35:** Miners in cage, Ian Pope; **Page 35:** Coal uses, Ursula Hurst; **Page 36:** Child miners, KGPA Ltd / Alamy Stock Photo; **Page 36:** Add Hod boy print, Scanpix/Creative Commons; **Page 36:** Carving of hod boy, Cheryl Mayo; **Page 36:** Old coalminers, Ursula Hurst; **Page 37:** Pit ponies, Ralph Anstis; **Page 37:** Union Pit monument, Cheryl Mayo; **Page 37:** Freeminer, Monument Colliery; **Page 38:** Squatter's cabin, Helen Sandford; **Page 38:** Lydbrook hillside, Dean Heritage Centre; **Page 39:** Inside miner's cottage, Courtesy Lightmoor Press; **Page 39:** Children at well, Bernard Kear; **Page 39:** Girl on loo, Bernard Kear; **Page 40:** Cinderford High St, Dean Heritage Centre; **Page 40:** Westaway shop, Dean Heritage Centre; **Page 41:** Pannage, British Library, Public domain, via Wikimedia Commons; **Page 41:** Sheep on road, Jaggery/Creative Commons; **Page 41:** Town donkey, Ursula Hurst; **Page 42:** Barge, John Powell; **Page 42:** Lydney Harbour, Dean Heritage Centre; **Page 42:** Old Severn Bridge, Helen Brodbin; **Page 43:** Toll house, Alan Everett; **Page 43:** Tramway with horses, Cyril Hart collection courtesy Glos Archives; **Page 43:** Painting of steam train, Tom Bint; **Page 43:** Map of railways 1880, Ursula Hurst; **Page 43:** Dean Forest Railway logo, Dean Forest Railway; **Page 44:** Rural poverty 1700s, Chronicle / Alamy Stock Photo; **Page 44:** Overcrowded houses, Classic Image / Alamy Stock Photo; **Page 44:** Workhouse, iStock.com/ilbusca; **Page 45:** Victorian children, © Look and Learn; **Page 45:** Mounted police 1926 strike, Dean Heritage Centre; **Page 46:** Old cannon ball, Martin Bergsma/Shutterstock.com; **Page 46:** Battle of Coleford, David Broadbent / Alamy Stock Photo;
Page 47: Mosquito aircraft in flight, BlueBarronPhoto/Shutterstock.com; **Page 47:** Lumberjills , Ruth Fletcher; **Page 47:** Italian PoW football team, Laura Porciani; **Page 48:** Poachers with deer, Ursula Hurst;
Page 49: Speech House , Dean Heritage Centre; **Page 49:** Helen Sandford drawing, Helen Sandford;
Page 49: Warren James mural, Wendy Conway / Tom Cousins; **Page 50:** Quarry, Nick Miller;
Page 50: Fishermen with salmon, John Powell; **Page 50:** Putcher, John Powell; **Page 50:** Gold mine, Dean Heritage Centre; **Page 51:** Ruspidge Utd, Jackie Sannwald ; **Page 51:** Pillowell Silver Band, Dave Powell ;
Page 51: Fancy dress parade, David Baldwin; **Page 51:** Children with hoops, Bernard Kear;
Page 52: Victorian school, Averil Kear; **Page 52:** Dunce hat and cane, Ursula Hurst; **Page 52:** Viney Hill School 1916, June Love; **Page 52:** Viney Hill School 1948, Rosemary Cleworth; **Page 52:** Viney Hill School 1965, Roger Smith; **Page 53:** HOOF leaf logo, Viv Hargreaves; **Page 53:** Rally poster, Helen Sandford;
Page 53: Photo of 3 murals, Tom Cousins / Helen Conway; **Page 53:** Not for Sale sign, Liza Gough Daniels; **Page 54:** Stained glass sculpture, Sue Middleton; **Page 54:** Bike rider, Forestry England;
Page 55: Winifred Foley, Jennifer Townsend; **Page 55:** Singing Detective, sjvinyl / Alamy Stock Photo;
Page 55: Writers mural, Sue Middleton; **Page 56:** Dean Heritage Centre , Dean Heritage Centre;
Page 56: Clearwell Caves map, Jonathan Wright; **Page 56:** Hopewell Colliery tunnel, John French ;
Page 56: Steam train, Adrian Copley ; **Page 57:** Scenes of Childhood cover, Bernard Kear ;
Page 57: children playing, Bernard Kear; **Page 58:** Lightmoor Colliery, Dean Heritage Centre;
Page 58: Clearwell Caves, Jonathan Wright; **Page 58:** Horses, Forestry England;
Page 58: Freemining today, Mark Ward; **Page 59:** Flour Mill Colliery, Mark Rodway; **Page 59:** Oak tree felling, Dean Heritage Centre; **Page 59:** Chainsaw, Forestry England **Page 60:** Ursula Illustrator, Ursula Hurst

Flour Mill Colliery, Bream

Felling an oak tree before the invention of the chainsaw

Felling with a chainsaw

About the author

Andy Seed is the author of over 30 books, including the popular memoir series *All Teachers Great and Small* for adults, and the international bestseller *The Clue is in the Poo* for children, a guide to tracks and signs of animals. In 2015 he won the Blue Peter Book Award and is the proud owner of the show's legendary badge. Now based in the Forest, Andy spends much of his time visiting schools and festivals, inspiring children to read.

Find out more at
www.andyseed.com

For details of talks for groups of all ages email
andy@andyseed.com

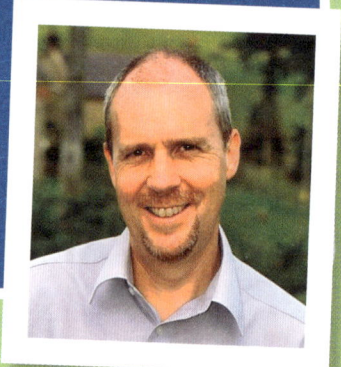

About the illustrator

Ursula Hurst is an artist specialising in children's illustrations, based in Lancashire.

When she's not drawing on her iPad with her scruffy dog at her feet, she can be found in schools running art workshops, coordinating community festivals or up a ladder painting murals.

For further information visit www.artdaze.co.uk, or email ursula@artdaze.co.uk

Forest of Dean Local History Society

This book is sponsored by the Forest of Dean Local History Society. The Society, founded in 1948, has some 300 members who enjoy an annual programme of monthly talks, history-related walks and visits. Both its annual journal, *The New Regard*, and its quarterly newsletter have won national awards.

Visit www.forestofdeanhistory.org.uk

Find out more

In addition to visiting Dean Heritage Centre and the other places listed above, you can borrow books for free from your local library. Forest libraries have a local history section full of information and pictures.

Useful websites
www.sungreen.co.uk
An excellent collection of old photos of the Forest

forest-of-dean.net
The Forest of Dean Family History Trust: good for finding out about ancestors

www.deanweb.info/history
A collection of all kinds of pictures and facts

Patter puzzle answer
Here is the meaning of *"Thee'st needn't gyule, thee duss knaw I was vust."*:

"You don't need to sneer, you know I was first."

Also by Andy Seed: Look out for The Wildlife of the Forest, *coming soon.*